CW00688788

Royal
Botanic Garden
Edinburgh

THE YEW HEDGE

Conserving ancient trees from the UK and beyond

Martin Gardner

Illustrated by
Jacqui Pestell and Sharon Tingey

MIX
Paper from
responsible sources
FSC® C115556

1056914
Printed on Carbon Captured paper

Printed by McAllister Litho Glasgow Ltd

ISBN: 978-1910877-42-5

© Royal Botanic Garden Edinburgh, 2022.
Published by the Royal Botanic Garden Edinburgh
20A Inverleith Row, Edinburgh, EH3 5LR

rbge.org.uk

All rights reserved. No part of this publication may be reproduced,
stored in a retrieval system or transmitted, in any form, or by any means,
electronic, mechanical, photocopying, recording or otherwise,
without the prior written consent of the copyright holders and publishers.

Proceeds from sales of this book will be used to support the work of the
Royal Botanic Garden Edinburgh.

The Royal Botanic Garden Edinburgh is a Non Departmental Public Body (NDPB)
sponsored and supported through Grant-in-Aid by the
Scottish Government's Environment and Forestry Directorate (ENFOR).

The Royal Botanic Garden Edinburgh is a
Charity registered in Scotland (number SC007983).

Edited by Elanor Clarke, Alice Young and Erica Schwarz
Designed by Caroline Muir
Assisted by Andrew Lindsay

Contents

Introduction

Around 15 years ago an idea triggered a project of astonishing scope which turned the ordinary into something extraordinary. At the Royal Botanic Garden Edinburgh a hedge surrounds the Edinburgh Garden which is home to some of the world's most threatened species, enclosing and protecting these important and beautiful plants. Perhaps in a place such as this, and with the unique skills of the staff who work there, this hedge could become something more than simply a hedge: it could itself become part of the story.

This thought developed into a unique project to help conserve the European yew (*Taxus baccata*). Over several years horticulturists and scientists worked together to collect and cultivate almost 2,000 trees to form not just a boundary but a genetic resource to safeguard diversity in this important conifer species for the long term. The plants for the hedge were collected from 13 countries where this species, sometimes also referred to as the English or common yew, is threatened, and 36 sites throughout Britain and Ireland where it is cultivated.

A hedge is a perfect metaphor, a collection of individuals forming a complete whole, a coming together of separate parts for a common goal. Through the undertaking of this project, collecting the plants to form the physical hedge, we collected something else too, an important body of stories, history and folklore from different countries and cultures, a bank of information as important as the genetic material which must too be protected. Here, in this small book, is that united story, an important history of ancient oral accounts, tales of extraordinary longevity, pagan worship, intriguing legends, myths and stories intricately woven into regional folklore, inseparable from the modern-day plight of this ancient and mystical plant.

THE PROJECT

The inaugural planting of the Yew Conservation Hedge took place on 8th April 2014. It was undertaken by the Reverend Anne Brennan, from Fortingall Parish Church. This first planting originated from cuttings taken from the famous Scottish Fortingall Yew, one of the oldest and most historic trees in Britain, if not Europe.

The project was led by the Royal Botanic Garden Edinburgh's International Conifer Conservation Programme (ICCP) in collaboration with the Garden's Horticultural Department. Under the supervision of the ICCP, Tom Christian, who has a special interest in conifers, conducted a pilot study of the hedge as part of an Honours Degree of BSc in Horticulture with Plantsmanship at the Royal Botanic Garden Edinburgh, which also involved collection of propagation material from many of the yew trees.

One of the most compelling elements of the project from these beginnings has been the involvement of Royal Botanic Garden Edinburgh staff from across the institution, especially those who are nationals of the countries where the yew is native. To this end, Albanian Agron Shehi, Danish Axel Poulsen and Croatian Vlasta Jamnický were able to make collections of yews from their own native countries. In addition, Horticulture staff who were familiar with locations where some of the yews occurred played an important role in the collection of seed and cuttings from those places. For example, William Hinchliffe, who hails from south-west England, collected from a native population in Devon, and Richard Brown, who had prior valuable experience carrying out field work in Western Asia and Eastern Europe, collected from native populations in Georgia, Russia and Ukraine.

It is highly appropriate that this wide contribution established a hedge that physically embraces the Garden, and relates intrinsically to the Royal Botanic Garden Edinburgh's remit of international collaboration in conserving biodiversity in the face of global extinction.

Hedges

WHY PLANT A HEDGE?

It is perfectly reasonable to ask why the Yew Conservation Hedge is so important and why it was necessary to replace a holly hedge which had, for many years, perfectly fulfilled all the requirements for an amenity hedge. The holly hedge we replaced was comprised of a single clone, to ensure uniformity, and each autumn it received a routine cut to keep it neat and tidy. However, for the modern-day botanic garden, which specialises in curating ultra-high levels of biological diversity, maintaining a hedge with a single clone surely runs counter to its scientific strategy. Instead of a single clone of holly, the newly planted Hedge is crammed with genetic diversity and thus has the potential of contributing to the conservation of the European yew.

Although yew is slow-growing compared with many other hedging species, it is by far the best choice for a hedge. Yew has dense growth that substantially absorbs noise, it is low maintenance, requiring only one cut per year, and if the drainage is good, it will thrive in most soil conditions in full sun and in deep shade. Additionally, yew hedges are good for wildlife, providing both food and shelter for a wide variety of birds and insects. The Royal Botanic Garden Edinburgh's Yew Conservation Hedge differs from traditional hedgerows because it is not species-rich but, importantly, it is genetically diverse.

HEDGES: A SHORT HISTORY

The word hedge comes from the Anglo-Saxon name *gehaeg*, meaning enclosure. Hedges can be described as a continuous row of trees or shrubs, which are actively maintained to form a boundary or barrier, to prevent expansion into adjacent areas, providing some privacy and protection. Hedges can also be perfect places for wildlife, particularly for nesting birds, and also serve as barriers to sound and pollution, creating boundaries between properties, and even serving to deter unwanted visitors.

Hedges in Europe date back as far as the Bronze and Iron Ages, during which time they were used for containing livestock and later for marking parish boundaries, leading to the Enclosure Acts, which created legal property rights to areas of land that were previously common land. Historically, the commonest choice of species for hedges was hawthorn (*Crataegus monogyna*) because its thorn-clad stems were considered a good deterrent to straying farm animals, but also because its wood was traditionally used for making tool handles. Latterly, with the loss of so much woodland habitat, field hedges have taken on the important function of conservation corridors for wildlife, with species-rich hedges having an approved Habitat Action Plan under the UK Biodiversity Action Plan. Sadly, between 1945 and 1993 almost 50 per cent of British hedges were removed, mainly due to agricultural intensification. Today there is an active programme to reinstate hedges.

YEW THE CONIFER

It may come as a surprise that yews are conifers. They are very unusual conifers because instead of having the familiar seed-bearing woody cones of a pine or a spruce, they bear cones which imitate fruits or berries – *baccata* from the yew's Latin name means berry bearing. All plants have evolved to have the most effective strategy for dispersing seed. The 'fruit' of the yew consists of a colourful scarlet fleshy structure (known as an aril), which partly encloses the seed. Fruit-eating birds digest the highly nutritious, sweet-tasting flesh, but crucially not the seed, which is very poisonous. In this way the seed passes through the bird unharmed so that it can eventually germinate, hopefully some distance away from the mother tree. Yews also have male and female reproductive structures on separate plants to promote out-pollination.

The yews comprise about 12 species, mostly distributed in the northern hemisphere from Alaska to Japan, but some species do occur in the tropics in South-East Asia. The European yew is mainly distributed in Europe, with other native populations occurring in Morocco, Iran and the Caucasus, as well as a very small population in the Azores.

YEW THE HEALER

Many may be surprised to learn that even though most parts of
the yew are extremely poisonous, for centuries it has been used for
healing purposes. Since the early Middle Ages, yew preparations
were used in a wide range of treatments, including medicines for
arthritis, diphtheria, epilepsy, parasites, rheumatism and tonsilitis.
Unsurprisingly though, overdosing on yew preparations sadly led
to the untimely death of countless patients. More recently, in the
mid-1960s, a revolutionary discovery was made in the USA, when
an anti-cancer activity was identified. Today Taxol (the brand name
for Paclitaxel) is recognised as one of the most successful cancer
drugs ever produced. Interestingly, one of the oldest preserved texts
of ancient Indian medicine, dating back to the first half of the
6th century, mentions a treatment for abdominal cancer containing
parts of the yew. It seems it has taken the West 1,400 years to
rediscover the lifesaving anti-cancer properties of the tree.

YEW THE POISONER

Beware! The Yew Conservation Hedge is poisonous; most parts are capable of killing animals and humans by causing cardiac arrest due to the presence of taxine alkaloids. For millennia, yew alkaloids were used as a method of suicide and a chemical weapon during hunting and warfare. It is said that even sleeping beneath the shade of a yew tree was once considered to be dangerous.

Perhaps it is quite alarming that a public garden should choose to plant a hedge that is so potentially poisonous to its visitors, human or animal! However, we should not be too alarmed because most public gardens, even if they don't cultivate yew trees, grow many plants that are equally poisonous. For example, daffodils, lily of the valley, wisteria and even the leaves of rhubarb have very poisonous properties. Like so many other plants, the yew has a lethal chemical arsenal to prevent it from being eaten by insects and other animals. The amount of plant material needed to produce a lethal dose is surprisingly small: 50–100 grams of leaves will be fatal to humans, and only 30 grams to horses and pigs. However, it is very common to see yew browsed by deer and livestock without any apparent harm; roe deer in particular can build up immunity to the toxic effects of yew. Certainly, I have seen countless examples whereby yew trees are browsed.

HERITAGE YEW TREES

Britain and Ireland have inherited the greatest number of old yews in the world. The Ancient Yew Group, which champions the recording and preservation of Britain and Ireland's important yew trees, lists 1,500 trees on their website. Due to the enormous choice available, the task of prioritising heritage trees for the Hedge proved to be quite daunting. Criteria such as extreme age, inspiring historical tales and novel modern-day uses were used in short-listing the 37 trees that have been planted in the Hedge. In all, 17 trees from Scotland, 13 from England, three from Wales and four from the island of Ireland were chosen. Our belief that most heritage yew trees could represent local native genetic material which is now otherwise extinct, and the subsequent inclusion of this in the Hedge, is potentially of great benefit for the conservation of the European yew.

WHY CHURCHYARDS?

The planting of yews was part of a tradition that predates the arrival of Christianity to the British Isles. Sixty-seven per cent of all large-girthed yew trees are found in churchyards; hence many churchyard trees feature in the Hedge. The yew was considered a natural emblem of eternity in the Druidic tradition of reincarnation, and later the Christian doctrine used it as a powerful symbol of resurrection, which remains today. It is said that some English churches were established on sites of pagan worship, where yews were planted, in order to Christianise the sites; however, this theory has been challenged by some. There have been many theories addressing why yews are planted in churchyards; some are clearly very implausible, such as that they thrived on corpses, or one suggestion that yew absorbed the vapours produced by putrefaction.

Whatever the reason, the yew is very decorative with its evergreen foliage, and the longevity of the trees themselves was used as a symbol of everlasting life. It is important to note that when sites were being designated for pagan worship, or as churches, there were very few or no other suitable evergreen trees to choose from; perhaps in Scotland the only other contender could have been the native Scots pine, but its longevity credentials were not in the same league.

Sadly around ten per cent of large yew trees have been lost from churchyards, mostly over the last 100 years. These losses have occurred due to felling on health and safety grounds, vandalism and storms. Although Tree Preservation Orders (TPOs) afford some protection to individual trees, there is no current legislation in place, which gives adequate protection to heritage trees in the UK.

Conservation groups such as The Ancient Tree Forum and the Woodland Trust are calling for the equivalent to Scheduled Ancient Monument status to be applied to old and historic trees.

AGEING HERITAGE YEWS

The inflated ages given for heritage yew trees, sometimes ranging from 3,000 to 7,000 years, are often driven by sensational media headlines rather than being based on good science. However, the task of ageing trees is complex, especially as most old yew trees have hollow centres, making a count of growth rings impossible. Currently, the only precise way to determine the age of a tree is to count the annual tree rings from a trunk section, or that of standing trees by using a hand-driven increment corer, which intersects the pith of the tree.

Around the year 2000, a rare opportunity arose when a yew tree in the churchyard of St Mary's Church, West Horsley, had to be felled due to its close proximity to the church. The 2.8-metre circumference of the solid trunk yielded an annual growth ring count of 313 years.

It was then possible to compare this with a well-known methodology for estimating the ages of yew trees when coring is not an option, which gave an age of 253 years, underestimating the true age by 19 per cent. One cannot necessarily extrapolate known ages and apply them to, say, a tree of twice the girth, and assume that it will be twice the age. Local environmental variabilities have to be taken into consideration, factors like soil type, climate etc.

Members of The Ancient Yew Group, together with other dendrochronologists (experts in ageing trees), are continuing to make progress towards a more accurate methodology for ageing yew trees. Until this happens, it is thought that an age of around 2,000 years for some of our oldest yews is likely. In 2010, The Ancient Yew Group proposed a new classification for old yew trees, based on age, trunk girth and significance. The four categories used are: Notable (300–500 years), Veteran (500–800 years), Ancient (800–1,200 years), and Exceptional (1,200 or more years).

Native yews in the Hedge

The European yew can be found throughout most of Europe to western Asia (Iran) and North Africa (Algeria and Morocco) in 45 different countries. In the UK it has a restricted distribution, with classic woodlands occurring on the South and North Downs in south-east England. It also occurs on limestone outcrops in the north-east, and North Wales. It is doubtful if its occurrence in Scotland is truly wild, as throughout much of its range extensive planting has sometimes caused confusion regarding its native distribution. The species has experienced a sharp decline throughout its natural geographical range and although not considered globally threatened, it is nationally listed as threatened in many of the countries where it is native. The Yew Conservation Hedge includes yews from 17 countries; many of these populations are under considerable threat.

In choosing the countries to collect from, we were trying to represent the geographic extremities of yew's natural distribution. We targeted the northernmost population from northern Norway, the southernmost forests of the Rif Mountains of Morocco, and the westernmost forests of Ireland. Plans to collect from the most eastern population of the Hyrcanian Forests, which border the Caspian Sea coast in northern Iran, were thwarted due to Foreign Office security restrictions. Other collections were not successful; for example, those from Estonia failed due to seedling die-off, and the Turkish collections proved to have extremely poor germination. All collections were made in the form of seed from several individuals, in order to represent broad genetic sampling, which for conservation purposes is crucial.

NATIVE YEWS UNDER THREAT

Needless to say, browsing pressure on natural stands of yew by deer and rabbits can cause serious conservation problems, especially for the establishment of seedlings. Historically, the toxicity to cattle and horses led to the extermination of the European yew from many woodland habitats, which were used for grazing animals. Today an additional pressure on yew has been the discovery of the anti-cancer drug Paclitaxel (see p. 6), which has led to the uncontrolled harvesting of all yew species worldwide in order to supply the global demand, although the European yew may be at less risk compared with Asian yew species. Nevertheless, its very attractive wood, which is among the hardest of all the softwood species, has made it one of the most highly prized woods of all temperate trees, and this has led to over-exploitation in much of its natural range.

One of the earliest and most widespread uses of the wood was for making longbows. In 1991, a hillwalker found a longbow in a peat bog known as Rotten Bottom, on a remote, boggy plateau in the Scottish Borders; the bow is thought to be 6,000 years old. There were extensive trade routes across Europe in order to feed the great demand in England for the wood; the main trading partners were the lands in present-day Germany and Austria targeting the higher-altitude, slow-growing yew trees, which had a tight grain. Such was the destruction that yew is a great rarity in the Tyrol today. Some of the greatest destruction occurred in the Carpathians in the 17th and 18th centuries, when the local Hutsul people paid taxes in yew trees, which resulted in 37,800 trees being felled.

HABITAT

The European yew normally occurs as single trees or in relatively small groups. However, throughout its natural range it can form large stands of many thousands of individuals. Although it favours limestone substrates, even growing on chalk in southern England, yews can tolerate most soil types, even acid soils with a high peat content. It prefers well-drained soils, but can cope with seasonal flooding, although it is susceptible to long-term poor drainage. In the north of its range, including the UK, it is tolerant of prolonged periods of sub-zero temperatures and whilst it has a moderate tolerance of drought conditions, it prefers oceanic climates with moderate temperatures. Yew normally grows at low altitude, whereas in the Mediterranean region it only occurs at high, mountainous elevations. In the Caucasus it grows from sea level to over 2,000 metres in altitude. Notably, yew is very shade tolerant and often occurs under the canopy of dense forest, especially beech trees. However, for good regeneration the seedlings are not as shade tolerant and require lighter conditions.

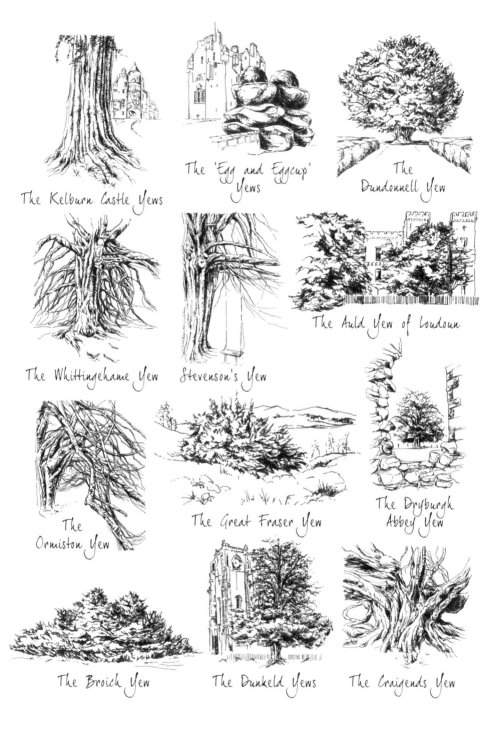

The Kelburn Castle Yews

The 'Egg and Eggcup' Yews

The Dundonnell Yew

The Whittingehame Yew

Stevenson's Yew

The Auld Yew of Loudoun

The Ormiston Yew

The Great Fraser Yew

The Dryburgh Abbey Yew

The Broich Yew

The Dunkeld Yews

The Craigends Yew

John Knox's Yew

The Malleny Yews

Robert the Bruce's Yew

The Fortingall Yew

The Traquair Yew

Scotland

The native conifers of Scotland include Scots pine and juniper, but what about the widely occurring yew tree, surely it has to be native? Alas, for 300 years or more passionate debate, and even dedicated research involving the analysis of sedimentary pollen records, has failed to give conclusive evidence that yew is truly native to Scotland. With just over 100 trees, it is surprising how relatively few planted heritage yews are recorded for Scotland – compare this with the English county of Hampshire, which has over 270 trees. Nevertheless, for the Yew Conservation Hedge, there was plenty of choice from yews with compelling stories. These include trees from religious sites, stately homes, wild landscapes of the Highlands and even one tree nestled by a small stream and overlooked by an ever-expanding housing estate.

The Craigends Yew

This yew is an outstanding example of a layering yew tree. Its branches gradually lower to the ground, where they develop roots and send up robust shoots that eventually grow into independent trees. This is often referred to as a 'walking yew', and this example is thought to be the largest of its kind in Scotland. Its location, near to Houston in Renfrewshire, is today in the middle of a sprawling housing estate, and therefore must be one of the more unusual locations for an ancient yew tree. Estimates put it at between 500 and 700 years old and, because of its layering habit, the clones could live for evermore!

Any thoughts that this would be a straightforward tree to track down were soon dispelled when our search began – locate the housing estate and then it will be easy to find an imposing, sprawling evergreen tree, we thought. Not so. Instead it proved to be quite elusive – even within a short distance of its location, next to the River Gryffe. Its low, sprawling habit makes it almost hidden from view and camouflaged by many other old yew trees. The river, with its wooded waterside margin, is like a green vein twisting its way through the estate and as such is a vital refuge for wildlife and a favourite habitat for yew trees. In places, the river has formed deep channels in the red sandstone bedrock; this is all clear to see when you cross the metal bridge from the adjacent housing estate.

The River Gryffe and the yew tree have lived in harmony for centuries – they have been inseparable. Like its neighbouring trees, the yew has helped to prevent flooding by holding back water, but importantly its roots act as a filtration system and have cleaned the water. The river, which flows for about 26 kilometres and eventually runs into the Black Cart Water near to Glasgow International Airport, once powered the watermills at Kilmalcolm and Crosslee. Since 1973, the immediate surroundings of the river and its famous yew tree have seen a dramatic transformation when the first houses started to be built as part of a series of housing estates. Prior to this, the area formed part of the Craigends Estate and was home to the Cunninghame family. Craigends Mansion House was a very large and impressive building dating back to the 15th century. Lady Cunninghame, the last owner of the estate, passed it on to her nephew, who lacked the funding for its long-term upkeep. It soon fell into disrepair and was sold to a housing developer in the 1960s.

Unlike the other great layering yew trees of Scotland, for example at Broich, Ormistion and Whittingehame, the main trunk of the Craigends Yew has either collapsed or been coppiced, hence it has not formed an enclosed central cavern. With a spread of 40 metres, this multi-stemmed tree is indeed impressive. In 1890 the girth was measured at 6.4 metres and today this has increased to 8.68 metres. Rarely have I seen other plants growing on yew trees (these plants are known as epiphytes), but here there is an abundance of mosses, lichens, and ferns colonising this great survivor, which sadly is not in the best condition. Much of the foliage is showing signs of browning – let's hope this is no more than environmental stress rather than the effects of a debilitating plant pathogen. Furthermore, this tree has been excessively pruned – the key to maintaining yew trees is to restrict pruning to the bare minimum and only when absolutely necessary, for example, when limbs are in danger of causing personal harm.

The tree straddles a walkway, which means that soil compaction could be a stress-causing factor. Because of its accessibility, it has become a popular meeting point – there is clear evidence of antisocial behaviour, which includes fire damage and the obligatory litter associated with modern-day outdoor life. However, many people in the local community respect and care for this remarkable tree. In 2016, the Craigends Yew was entered for the Tree of the Year competition after a local woman contacted the Woodland Trust in her quest to increase local recognition for the tree. The entry came second in the competition for the Scottish Tree of the Year and as a result of the publicity there has been a lot more local interest. In 2018, a conservation programme removed several nearby trees to reduce shading and cleared much of the surrounding invasive scrub. A new information sign is being made, and it is hoped that the tree's future has been secured. Profile-raising of these old yew trees is incredibly important, but sometimes doing so can increase visitor traffic, which often has a detrimental effect on the tree through soil compaction, litter and vandalism. We have to find a way of celebrating these trees without causing them long-term damage.

The Broich Yew

Dominating the driveway entrance to Broich House – a private dwelling near the picturesque village of Kippen in Stirlingshire – stands another of Scotland's famous yew trees. In common with others, it is not of any great height, only 13 metres tall, but is celebrated for its layering branches, which have given the tree an enormous spread, and today its circumference measures an impressive 120 metres. Because of its location, it is perhaps one of Scotland's least-known ancient yew trees; however, it has been here for a very long time – some say it could be over 600 years old.

We should applaud the many generations who have occupied Broich House for letting this magnificent tree express its true character and allowing its branches to expand ever outwards without intervention. The most recent occupant, the late Sir Peter Hutchinson, Former Chair of the Royal Botanic Garden Edinburgh Board of Trustees and Chair of the Forestry Commission (now known as Forestry and Land Scotland), was a great champion of this notable tree. Sir Peter was a passionate, and very knowledgeable, dendrologist, having travelled through much of the temperate world in pursuit of trees and shrubs. He was very proud of the yew tree and spoke of it with great verve; because of his association with the Garden, it is very fitting that this tree forms part of the Hedge.

There is little documentation associated with this tree, so many questions still remain unresolved. Why was it planted, could it have been part of a ceremonial planting, and what is its true age? Claims that it was planted by the monks from the nearby Inchmahome island in the Lake of Menteith relate to the fact that during the 12th century they once owned the Broich property. The monks would have been associated with other old trees as there are three sweet chestnuts, reputed to be 400 years old, on the island.

Robert Hutchinson, in his paper 'On the old and remarkable yew trees in Scotland' published in the *Transactions of the Scottish Arboricultural Society* (1890), gives a height of 10.7 metres with a girth of 4.5 metres (measured 0.3 metres from ground level) for the tree. More recently the girth measurement was recorded as 3.86 metres (measured 1.2 metres from ground level). The trunk appears to be entire with no hollowing, which can be a characteristic of much older trees. Today the yew is in excellent condition, forming a perfectly proportioned tree with branches sweeping to the ground and forming an impenetrable skirt with no obvious way in. Once inside the dark and gloomy chamber, formed by the descending branches twisting and looping as they fall to the ground, it is worth reminding oneself that this massive conglomeration of branches and foliage is indeed from a single tree. The Ancient Yew Group classify this tree as being 'Notable', which places its age between 300 and 500 years. Whatever its age, this is one of Scotland's most remarkable yew trees.

The Dryburgh Abbey Yew

S tanding in the grounds of Dryburgh Abbey on the banks of
the River Tweed, near to Melrose in the Scottish Borders,
is one of Scotland's oldest yews, said to have been planted
by monks in 1136. This historic religious site is not only home to a
noteworthy yew tree, but is also the burial ground of Sir Walter Scott,

one of Scotland's most famous novelists. However, like most abbeys, it hasn't always been a peaceful place of worship and meditation, for it bears the scars of pillage and terrible destruction.

The ages of yew trees are subject to much debate and certainly the Dryburgh tree is no exception. The claim that monks planted the tree in 1136 has it predating the abbey by some 15 years. However,

Dr John Lowe (1830–1902), in his seminal work, *The Yew Trees of Great Britain and Ireland* (1897), poured doubt on this possibility. Based on the tree's growth measurements, Lowe concluded it to be no more than 300 years old. However, historical records of growth rates have been carefully examined by the Borders Forest Trust, which show this to be an extremely slow-growing tree and that an age of 900 years is indeed possible. With my own recent girth measurement of 3.80 metres, (1 metre above the ground), one would be forgiven for concluding a much younger age, as most trees of 900 years have a girth twice the size and would most likely be hollow.

This well-proportioned tree, with its remarkably straight bole, is located to the north-west of the ruinous abbey, on the edge of surrounding woodland. Like many of the trees in the abbey grounds, it is a favourite roosting place for bats – in fact three species have been recorded there. It is appropriate that these protected species are afforded sanctuary on this yew tree, as bats are associated with old-growth trees and ancient woodlands. It is heartening to see the yew tree guarded by a fence to prevent human foot traffic; however, there are clear signs that some branches have been cut. Arboriculturists or over-zealous horticulturists armed with pruning equipment are not ideal bedfellows for yew trees. As mentioned, unless there are exceptional circumstances, yew trees should not be pruned and instead allowed to extend their branches, which will eventually fall to the ground where they will root and send up new upright stems. This strategy allows yew trees to reach great ages. It is ironic that the yew is so celebrated for its longevity, when it is so often rudely shortened by unnecessary intervention.

During the 18th and 19th centuries the Dryburgh Yew witnessed great changes to the tree-cover of the abbey grounds. David Steuart Erskine, 11th Earl of Buchan (1742–1829), who bought the abbey in the 1780s, decided to enhance the grounds and surrounding landscape by planting a collection of exotic trees. This tradition has continued up to the present day; however, none of the relatively fast-growing trees, including the giant redwood from North America or the Atlas cedar from Morocco, will be able to outlive the slow-growing yew tree. The Earl of Buchan was also responsible for planting another yew tree, which grows in the south of the abbey grounds. This was noted by John Lowe, who refers to a tablet of stone on the north side of the Erskine burial ground, which states that the Earl of Buchan planted the tree in 1789.

If indeed the Dryburgh Yew has stood for 900 years, then it will have witnessed some disturbing events. The abbey, which stands on an elevated peninsula formed by a loop of the River Tweed, took over a century to build. It stood intact for only about 70 years before the first of four savage attacks took place. Perhaps the most notable was in 1322, when the monks celebrated the defeat in Scotland of Edward II's army by ringing the abbey bells. On hearing the bells, the enraged retreating army attacked the abbey, and torched the building. Dryburgh was not the only abbey they had plundered during their incursion to Scotland; nearby Melrose Abbey and the Abbey of Holyrood in Edinburgh were also badly damaged. Despite its close proximity to the main ruins, the yew tree has survived any lasting damage as a result of these many catastrophic attacks.

The Dundonnell Yew

D undonnell House, which is nestled at the head of a
sheltered valley with Little Loch Broom and overlooked
by An Teallach, has a most dramatic site for a house and
garden. To complete the perfect scene here in Wester Ross, there is
a meandering mountain watercourse forming the garden's southern
boundary. The setting for a beautiful mansion house, overlooking
an exquisite walled garden, could not be better. The walled
garden is laid out in a classical style, with a central path lined with

yew hedges and backed by lawns. The central piece is the most enormous and perfectly shaped yew tree, thought to be in excess of 300 years old.

Travelling over a largely treeless landscape to Dundonnell towards Ullapool and the west coast, it may strike you as perhaps the last place one would expect to find a very old yew. This is a remote part of the Western Highlands, known for its scenic splendour and with one of the lowest population densities in Europe. The final descent to the house runs adjacent to the Dundonnell River, where a narrow rocky gorge forms the spectacular Falls of Measach. Dundonnell is situated on the east bank of the river. The beautiful, tall, two-storey-and-attic mansion house is approached through a gate in the stone dyke. The estate originally belonged to the MacDonnell's of Glengarry, but by 1740 the Mackenzie family took ownership and built the original white-harled house.

Views across the walled garden invariably include the massive, 20-metre-tall yew tree and a nearby very large holly. Most of the garden has been created since 1956 – originally, in the mid-18th century, there was a walled enclosure and the walls were heightened in the early 19th century. The yew has a perfectly dome-shaped canopy with an enormous spread of 20 metres; equally impressive is its trunk with a girth of seven metres. The favourable fertile, alluvial soils are well drained, which helps to abate an annual rainfall of up to two metres. However, the winter temperatures can be as low as $-23°C$ and although this can cause browning of the tips of the branches, they always seem to recover in the spring.

What is unusual is that a tree at this latitude (57° N) has been able to reach such enormous proportions. Surprisingly, this remarkable tree has often failed to appear in the myriad of yew books published in recent years, and is even omitted from authoritative websites on Scottish yews. However, it is featured in the beautifully illustrated book *Heritage Trees of Scotland* (Rodger et al. 2003) in which the authors rightfully make the observation that the Dundonnell Yew "appears to have been coppiced many years ago and the resulting re-growth has formed a ring of interlaced stems". Yet again, as with most yew trees, we are faced with the conundrum of trying to resolve its age, with estimates varying from 300 to 1,000 years. The Ancient Yew Group lists the Dundonnell tree as being 'Ancient'; this category is applied to trees of 800 years or more and those with a girth exceeding seven metres. No doubt speculation over its true age will continue.

The Head Gardener, Will Soos, who has so skilfully crafted the walled garden into one of Scotland's most cherished private gardens, has made an interesting observation of the yew tree. When Will first arrived at the garden in 2004, he was able to walk under the canopy of the tree; however, some 17 years later, because one of the main branches is much lower, this is no longer possible. The lowering of the branches and the hollowing of the main trunk are clear indications that this tree is preparing itself for the long-haul. Like so many yew trees growing in open positions, once they reach a certain age the branches start to lower towards the ground and, if allowed to do so, they become layered and eventually send up stout new shoots, which can form stately new trees. Branch layering will help to stabilise the tree in high winds and the hollowing of the main trunk gives a degree of flexibility. This tree, if given the opportunity, would eventually be capable of engulfing most of the walled garden!

The Dunkeld Yews

S cotland's famous historic cathedral city of Dunkeld, known
as the Gateway to the Highlands, is not only celebrated as
an ancient sacred place, but today is renowned for its stands
of monumental trees. Much of the tree planting is a remarkable
legacy of the 4th Duke of Atholl, known as the 'Planting Duke',
who forested a largely treeless landscape and made Perth & Kinross
the cradle of Scottish forestry. However, the yew trees around
Dunkeld Cathedral predate this activity, as they are thought to be

at least 400 years old; some say they even predate the cathedral, but perhaps this is based on wishful thinking.

For the tree enthusiast there is perhaps no better place in Scotland to visit than Dunkeld, and to explore its picturesque, forested environs. This green oasis is in the heart of the 'Perthshire Big Tree Country', so-called because the region has more champion trees than any other area of the UK. Standing on Telford's Bridge, which joins Birnham with Dunkeld across the River Tay, one can start to survey the skyline in search of some of the celebrated monumental trees on the north bank of the river, just beyond the cathedral. One of these, the Douglas fir, was introduced by David Douglas from western North America in the late 1700s; he was one of many plant collectors who risked their lives to search for new and interesting trees. Also visible beneath these exotic trees are the darker and smaller silhouetted yews in the cathedral grounds and beyond; these may be a third of the size, but they are probably twice the age.

Standing on the site of the former Culdee Monastery of Dunkeld, the grey sandstone cathedral dates back to 1260, but it was not completed until 1501. The cathedral is surrounded by yew trees, most of which are multi-stemmed, and shadow the building on all sides. Two of these were noted by Hutchinson in his seminal paper of 1890. He says of the one close to the west gable of the cathedral that "[it has a] stiff upright habit of growth" and suggested that it resembles the Neidpath Yew (*Taxus baccata* 'Neidpathensis'), which was first recorded from Neidpath Castle in the Scottish Borders. The second yew tree, which stands close by, Hutchinson mentions as being quite different and describes it as a "peculiar-looking round-headed tree in full vigour".

The two yew trees from which cuttings were taken for the Yew Conservation Hedge stand outside of the grounds, just behind the cathedral, in what has become known as Cathedral Grove.

These trees are in good company for this is where some of the county's largest and most interesting trees grow. The most famous is the parent larch (*Larix decidua*), the sole survivor of the original five trees introduced from Europe and used by the 4th Duke of Atholl in his extraordinary tree planting, which amounted to over 14 million trees covering 4,250 hectares. It is known as the parent larch because by chance it hybridised with the Japanese larch and gave rise to a hybrid, which became an important Scottish forestry tree. The two yew trees have perfect boles. The tree closest to the cathedral I have measured at 15 metres tall with a girth of 4.3 metres (at 1 metre from the ground), while the second tree is 17.5 metres tall with a girth of 5.5 metres (at 1.10 metres from the ground). Although neither show any sign of hollowing, their crowns are beginning to thin. As both trees are of similar girth compared to some of those in the cathedral grounds, they are perhaps of similar age, which is estimated as being 400 years.

The Dunkeld Yews stand alongside non-native conifers introduced to cultivation in the mid- 19th century; most of these hail from temperate rainforests of the Americas. One of these, *Fitzroya cupressoides*, planted in the Cathedral Grove during the last 15 years, is of particular interest as it is able to compete with the yew trees in the longevity stakes. Native to Argentina and Chile, this highly threatened conifer can live for over 3,000 years, and is planted here as part of a conservation programme involving the Royal Botanic Garden Edinburgh in partnership with Forestry and Land Scotland and the Perth and Kinross Countryside Trust. It is highly appropriate that these two species, renowned for their longevity, are here, cheek by jowl, hopefully to face the next few centuries together.

The Fortingall Yew

S tanding within the confines of a stone wall in the quiet churchyard of Fortingall Parish Church is the most visited and photographed tree in the British Isles. It is a remarkable location in a picturesque village, surrounded by lofty mountains at the foot of Glen Lyon in the Highlands of Scotland. The Fortingall Yew is of no great stature, but due to its reputed age – wildly ranging from 2,000 to 9,000 years – the tree is greatly revered throughout Europe, if not the world.

Undoubtedly, the Fortingall Yew is one of the most documented trees in the British Isles and thus we have remarkable insight into the conditions for the tree during the past 250 years. The Welsh traveller and naturalist Thomas Pennant was the first to write about the tree in his celebrated work *A Tour in Scotland* (1771). In 1769 he came across the tree and said of it "In Fortingall church-yard are the remains of a prodigious yew-tree, whole ruins measured fifty-six feet and a half in circumference" (16.80 metres). The sketch in his book clearly shows the tree almost divided into two, with the centre of the trunk decayed to the ground (although, as so often with old decaying yew trees, there appears to be copious amounts of regrowth from the trunk). So great was the gap, it is said that a local custom was for funeral processions, complete with horse-drawn carriages, to pass through the tree when entering the churchyard. In the same year yet another traveller, an English barrister named Daines Barrington, also visited the Fortingall Yew, but his measurement was slightly smaller at 52 feet (15.85 metres).

During the late 18th century, the Fortingall Yew was becoming much celebrated and as a result intriguing legends started to be linked to the tree. One included Pontius Pilate being born to a local woman, fathered by a Roman diplomat visiting a Pictish king. As a child, it was said, he played beneath the yew tree. Such legends and its great age attracted more and more travellers to visit the tree, and unfortunately this led to a trade in souvenirs made from its wood. Such was the demand, with large branches being lopped off, that a protective stone wall was built, encircling the tree. Today the wall still stands with the addition of iron railings to allow for viewing.

Instead of destroying these ancient sites, it was a policy of the Church to Christianise them by the building of churches. Certainly the tree predates the present white-harled church, which was only built in 1900–02, and indeed the earliest church, which dates back to the late 7th century. Fortingall has long been an important centre for Christian worship – Adamnan, Abbot of Iona from 679 to 704, is thought to have visited Fortingall. Crop marks suggest the existence of an early monastery on or close by to the site of today's church. Perhaps further evidence of a monastery is a hand bell dating from the 600s which today hangs near the pulpit of the church.

Much of the continuous fascination surrounding the Fortingall Yew centres on speculation about its age; certainly the popular media seem to have ages of 5,000 years or more 'etched in stone'. However, the general view is that the yew is most likely to be in excess of 2,000 years old but certainly no more than 3,000. Trunk girth measurements can be used to reveal an approximate age of old trees but the widely fragmented trunk of the Fortingall Yew prevents an accurate calculation. The only insight we have of the original circumference are trunk fragments that are today indicated by marker pegs, which give a measurement of 15 metres. A very revealing observation of the tree is from 1838 by The Reverend Robert McDonald, the minister of Fortingall, who wrote in *The New Statistical Account of Scotland* that the tree appears as two distinct trees. However, he says that when he first became minister in 1806 he heard from a local man, who was in his 80s, that when he was a schoolboy he remembers hardly being able to enter between the two tree fragments. McDonald went on to say, "now a coach and four may pass through them… the dilapidation was partly occasioned by the boys of the village kindling their Beltane at its roots". This was the tradition of lighting a bonfire at the Celtic festival of Beltane and continued in Fortingall until 1924.

In more recent years new information about the tree has come to light. Up until 2015 the tree was thought to be entirely male, but that year a branch bearing female cones was discovered. This is one of several examples of yew trees bearing both male and female cones on the same tree (the species is normally of a single sex). If this observation had been made of any other yew tree, there would not have been the slightest stir; such is the fame of the Fortingall Yew.

The Great Fraser Yew

Above Loch Ness, among the bracken and heather of native woodland, grows one of Britain's most remote yew trees, said to be 700 years or more old. This tree had great significance for the Stratherrick Frasers, who used it as a meeting point to gather beneath before they went into battle, proudly wearing a sprig of its foliage. Surrounded by a grove of suckering stems, the central mother tree is hollow and crumbling and looking the worse for wear as it enters the last chapter in a remarkable life.

Finding the Fraser Yew is quite a challenge, and only with permission and guidance from the Knockie Estate at Stratherrick should one make the strenuous trek of almost five kilometres over moorland on the south side of Loch Ness. Sadly I have never managed to experience the adventure of visiting this remarkable tree. Tom Christian, who collected cuttings for the Yew Conservation Hedge, described his perilous journey to the yew tree: "I had to negotiate heather moorland full of surreptitious bogs and burns, and deer fences until I finally descended an extremely steep slope that took me to the tree. At no time during the 'search and find' does one have sight of the tree as it is hidden in a hollow on the mountainside." One can imagine that this must have been the perfect hidden location for the gathering of Fraser clansmen before they went into battle.

The tree is perched on the western slopes of Beinn a'Bhacaidh, within a short distance of the loch shore on the precipitous slopes of the 'hill of hindrance'. The location is also significant because it has been designated a Site of Special Scientific Interest (SSSI) and lies within the Easter Ness Forest, which is biologically important for its upland ash and oak woodland. The tree is unique in that it is surrounded by about 20 younger yew trees, which originate from root suckers. Normally, an old tree such as this would regenerate and grow outwards by the side branches, gradually lowering and where they reach the ground new vertical shoots arising. The grove of suckering trees has an astonishing circumference of 110 metres, while the main central tree measures 4.58 metres in girth when measured at ground level. How long this tree has been growing here is difficult to ascertain due to the level of decay of the main trunk, but an estimate of 700 years is thought to be realistic.

Old yew trees served as a source of wood for making bows, with the main stave coming from the radius of the tree. It is said that the Stratherrick Frasers used to take the long trail down from Loch Knockie to the site of the tree and select wood for their longbows. There must have been other large yew trees in the area in order to supply enough timber for making longbows. It is also said that young men would "collect a plaid full of yew sprig for the expected

appearance of the Chief… or in more sombre times for gathering
to march to support Bonnie Dundee or Bonnie Prince Charlie".
Tartans became synonymous with the symbol of clan kinship and
clansmen were recognised by their tartan. However, there was
also recognition by the wearing of a plant badge on their bonnets.
For the MacDonalds this was heather, the Robertsons bracken,
and Clan Fraser wore a badge with the symbol of a yew.

Conjecture abounds as to the origin of this tree, but we will probably never be able to learn the truth. Generally, it is believed that a member of the Fraise family, which traces origins back to the French Provinces of Anjou and Normandy – the name is said to derive from the French word for strawberry, *fraise* – was responsible for planting the yew tree. What is of little doubt is that the rugged terrain of Beinn a'Bhacaidh and the remote location, which relatively few people manage to venture to, are contributing factors for the survival of this much- revered tree.

Today the tree still attracts Frasers from around the world, and a previous owner established a tradition of leaving a bottle of whisky hidden at the base of the tree, from which they would take a 'wee dram' to celebrate their arrival and perhaps to toast the tree's continued good health. There's also a box in which visitors can leave a message.

The Kelburn Castle Yews

The Kelburn Castle yew trees, located between Fairlie and Largs in North Ayrshire, are sheltered by luxuriant woodland on a hillside that gently slopes down to the Firth of Clyde. Cuttings for the Conservation Hedge were taken from two of these trees, which are said to be between 1,000 and

1,500 years old. They represent some of the most notable trees in a coastal landscape and in recent years have witnessed some colourful and controversial changes to the castle – urban art which has caused quite a stir among The Establishment!

The two trees stand about 20 metres apart and grow in the ornamental garden, where they are surrounded by well-maintained grounds with large expanses of lawns and colourful herbaceous borders. From here, a panoramic view is afforded across to the Isle of Great Cumbrae with the Isle of Bute in the background, and on a clear day the distinctive Paps of Jura are just visible far beyond. The West Coast of Scotland has a temperate maritime climate with typically warm, rather than hot, summers and cool to cold winters, which are ideal growing conditions for most conifers. However, heritage yew trees aren't commonly encountered in this part of Scotland; apart from the Kelburn Castle trees, there are only three other locations in Ayrshire with documented noteworthy trees.

Built in the 13th century, Kelburn Castle is the seat of the Earl of Glasgow and is claimed to be one of the oldest continuously inhabited homes in Scotland. It is likely that during this time yew trees will have been a prominent feature in the castle grounds. However, in recent years it is not only the yews that have made the headlines. In 2007, a team of Brazilian graffiti artists were contracted to decorate the walls and turrets of the south side of the castle. The mural features a psychedelic series of interwoven cartoons depicting surreal urban culture. In 2011, the mural was named as one of the world's top 10 examples of street art by author and designer Tristan Manco. It was heralded on a par with Banksy's work in Los Angeles and the Favela Morro Da Providencia in Rio de Janeiro. Despite this accolade, North Ayrshire Council reluctantly permitted the artwork on the understanding that it was temporary – the colourful mural still exists today!

The first tree to be encountered when entering the garden is dome-shaped and characteristically its branches almost stretch to the ground. If permitted to do so the branches will eventually root and throw up strong vertical growths, which will eventually grow into independent trees. Let's hope this tree will continue expanding and perhaps one day join the ranks of other celebrated Scottish trees, such as those at Ormiston and Whittingehame, which are aptly described as 'walking yews'. This is a female tree covered in autumn with cherry-red cones, and has a beautifully fluted trunk with a girth measurement of 5.34 metres at 1.5 metres from the ground. A few years prior to cuttings being taken from this tree, violent storms caused some damage to its canopy, but thankfully the tree has now fully recovered.

The second yew tree stands resplendent in an open position, again with a perfectly fluted trunk, and at 1.5 metres from the ground it has a girth measurement of just over six metres. Again this tree is female, yet some branches clearly have male flowers. The measurements of both trees suggest an age of between 500 to 600 years, which falls far short of the 1,000 and 1,500 years stated on a plaque in the castle grounds. Perhaps one day a more accurate estimate will be established, but in the meantime, we should admire these fine yew trees for their sheer beauty and stature, rather than their age. The two ancient Kelburn Yews are of such note that in 2002 they were included in the Forestry and Land Scotland's list of '100 Heritage Trees of Scotland'.

The Malleny Yews

Through a decorative wrought-iron gate, the formal walled garden of Malleny House opens out to a group of closely clipped yew trees known as the 'Four Evangelists'. This one-hectare garden is located on the outskirts of Edinburgh, to the south-east of Balerno. The 17th-century house, together with the garden and woodland, were gifted to the National Trust for Scotland in 1968.

The site where Malleny House and the surrounding lands stand today dates back to the early 14th century, with the earliest recorded ownership of the property being by the Knychtsoune family, in 1478. Four or five generations of this family owned the property until it was sold in 1617, after which there were numerous

successive owners. The present Malleny House was built in about
1637 by Sir James Murray of Kilbaberton who was Master of
Works to the Crown of Scotland.

It was not until the early 17th century that a group of 12 yew trees
known as the 'Twelve Apostles' were planted. Allegedly this planting
was to commemorate the 1603 Act of the Union between England
and Scotland. However, unlike the newly planted trees, which
established and flourished, the Act was not so successful, and it wasn't
until over a century later that the two countries were united by the
Acts of Union in 1707. Instead of allowing these yews to grow into
specimen trees, it was decided to clip them to form cones, which
skirted the ground. Today, the four remaining nine-metre-high trees
still have a similar shape, but instead of being clothed to the base,
they've been lifted to just over two metres above ground level.

Today yew trees dominate the woodlands that surround the main
garden. Although most are relatively recent plantings, a few individuals
look like contemporaries of the famous Twelve Apostles. In the main
garden, just behind the house, is a most unusual-shaped yew tree.
It is of no great stature or significant age, but it has branches that are
curiously contorted at right- angles. Perhaps this tree was once the
subject of topiary and since has grown out of its original shape?

Of the 12 original trees, eight were variously planted in the heath
bed near to the bowling green and in the azalea beds, all in close
proximity to the 1810 wing of the house. It was soon after the
Gore-Browne Henderson family bought the property in 1961 that
a decision was made to remove these trees, as they were casting
too much shade on the house. In her history of the house and
garden, published in 1976, Mrs Gore-Browne Henderson said of
this removal, "The Twelve [Apostles] were reduced to the Four
Evangelists by the Gore-Browne Hendersons with great benefit to

the house and garden". It has been said that the removal was carried out disregarding the legal mechanism, which protects significant trees, known as a Tree Preservation Order (TPO). One can perhaps understand the reasons for the removal of the trees, but with the ownership of the property being over a relatively brief period (1961–1968), after which the National Trust for Scotland took on the tenure, it is unfortunate that this unceremonious removal of the iconic yews took place. The Trust, which champions the protection of natural beauty and historic landscapes, will certainly feel a degree of regret that this signature planting had been so drastically diminished only seven years before they were gifted the property. However, plans are now in place to reinstate the original eight trees using propagation material from the remaining four.

Interestingly, the Malleny Yews are not the only historic planting that includes a group of 12 yew trees. The Great Court at Athelhampton House in Dorset has 12 trees shaped into perfect pyramids, which date back some 300 years. Topiary became popular in England in the 17th century, and the fashion for clipping trees and hedges (mostly of box, holly and yew), sometimes into fantastical shapes, became a very popular activity. The yew trees at Malleny House perhaps represent this fashion, and it is assumed that they were shaped into cones as soon as their size allowed, after they were planted in 1603. It is thought that the surviving four yew trees were always shaped, with their bases raised from the ground; certainly this is the case from images depicted in 1908.

In recent years, the trees have become misshapen due to a lack of annual trimming, and prior to 2014 one of the trees became badly damaged by the weight of excessive amounts of snow. In 2017 and 2020, drastic pruning took place so that once more these iconic trees can be restored to their former shape and size with a few more years' growth.

The Ormiston Yew

Located within a mile and a half of Ormiston village, near the site of Ormiston Hall in East Lothian, this remarkable tree, with its layering branches, is unlike any other yew tree in Scotland. The tree was well known as early as the 15th century, when it was recognised as a local landmark. A parchment dated

1474 and signed under the yew tree was discovered among old papers belonging to the Earl of Hopetoun. Today, the tree stands in what was once the garden of the magnificent Ormiston Hall, home to the Earl, which tragically burnt down in 1942.

The approach to the yew is across a small tree-lined meadow, through which one is guided by a well-worn path that leads to a relatively low, sprawling, dark green bank of branches covering an area slightly larger than a tennis court. If it were not for the path leading to a narrow break in the branches, then the first-time visitor would struggle to locate the tree. A very narrow entrance, via an outer veil of branches, leads to a highly specialised habitat that for hundreds of years has been cleverly crafted and controlled by the master of longevity – the yew tree. It is dark, but not too dark, with shafts of light piercing down through breaks in the tree's canopy. Here one is confronted by a network of radiating, serpent-like branches that have become layered to the ground and at which point 22, mostly upright, new trees have arisen. The tree is octopus-like, with a massive body, the trunk of which has recently been measured at just over five metres in circumference. From this, ten tentacle-like branches loop to the ground, stretching out to a distance of five metres either side of the main trunk. In places the surrounding ground is crowded with vertical growths; some are seedlings, but most have arisen from the layered branches. This growth formation is reminiscent of a tropical mangrove – similar to those saline woodlands, these yews have formed an intricate network of grounded branches, intermingled with new seedling recruits.

However, not all is at peace in this inner sanctum, for the tree has not always been allowed to continue its gradual encroachment of the surrounding meadow. The many metal supports placed under the branches over 100 years ago are evidence of this. These were intended to prevent the branches from falling to the ground

where they would have rooted to continue the ever-expansion
of this unique habitat, and many of the branches have been cut.
Over the years, obstructive branches have been removed to allow
visitors better access to the tree and now one side of the main
trunk is sadly devoid of the layered branches that makes this tree
so special. There are, in fact, three trees in this cavern-like habitat;
a second, considerably younger, tree has escaped such intervention
and is completely encircled by layered branches, which have
characteristically rooted and sent up strong new growths.

These trees occur on private land and the owners prefer a limited
number of visitors, especially due to the risk of harmful soil-borne
fungal pathogens being carried on shoes. Such is the concern that

when the public nominated 'The Great Ormiston Yew' for Scotland's Tree of the Year 2020 contest, a local resident insisted the tree should be withdrawn from the competition due to biosecurity concerns. Like so many conifer species, the common yew is susceptible to the root-killing fungus, *Phytophthora*. This aggressive water mould is not known for taking any prisoners; few infected trees will ever survive. Although yew trees have deep root systems, they also have a network of surface-feeding roots; soil compaction caused by trampling feet can impcde the soil porosity, which can be detrimental to trees. However, humans are not the only visitors to these yew trees – voracious deer constantly graze the new shoots arising from the layered branches and there is a clear grazing line on the branches skirting the outer part of the trees.

Some consider this a sacred place and in pre-Christian times it is likely that this tree was a meeting place for Scottish Druids – even today, a local group of Druids use this place for their ceremonies. Sometimes it is used as a wedding venue. However, one of the most famous visitors to this site was the Scottish clergyman, theologian and writer, John Knox (c.1514–1572), who was a leader of the Protestant Reformation and widely considered the founder of the Presbyterian denomination in Scotland. Born in nearby Haddington, Knox is reputed to have preached his early sermons within the canopy of the Ormiston Yew. It has been said that under the tree, Knox, along with his influential mentor George Wishart (1513–1546), sowed the seeds of the Reformation, which was ultimately to sweep throughout Scotland.

The age of The Great Ormiston Yew is often cited as 1,000 years, but this has been questioned by some, including the celebrated molecular biologist Dr Ulrich Loening. Ulrich together with his wife Francesca have acted as staunch guardians of the yew trees for over half a century and through their studies have concluded that the oldest of the three trees is likely to be about 750 years old.

Robert the Bruce's Yew

This very stunted and forlorn-looking tree stands in a private garden next to a white cottage at Stuc an T'Iobhairt, overlooking Loch Lomond between Inverbeg and Tarbet. Sadly, it is a shadow of its former self, which was noted not so much for its stature, but indeed thanks to a link with Scotland's national hero, Robert the Bruce (1274–1329). It is so famous that it is one of very few individual trees in Scotland to be mentioned on an Ordnance Survey map.

Bruce united the Scottish people against the English and re-established a fully independent Scotland, but eight years prior to becoming king of Scotland, in 1306, he was forced to escape across Loch Lomond from defeats in two ferocious battles, and take shelter under an ancient yew tree. His adversaries, led by the Earl of Pembroke and MacDougall of Lorne, were seeking revenge for the death of John Comyn, a former ally of Bruce, who in 1304 moved his allegiance over to Edward – this was viewed as an act of treachery and as a result Bruce killed him.

It is said that Bruce's crestfallen army traversed Loch Lomond in a boat that was taking in water and was only large enough to carry three men at a time – alas, it took 24 hours to ferry an army of 200 men across the loch. Eventually, they found shelter under the ancient yew tree at Stuc an T'Iobhairt (meaning the Hill of the Sacrifice), where Bruce rallied his low-spirited men. On their arrival Bruce stood under the tree raising their spirits. He used the yew to symbolise their struggle, heartily praising its strength and remarkable ability to endure. Eight years later, the fortunes of Bruce and his army changed by their winning the famous battle at Bannockburn, which led to independence. It is said that during this battle many of his fighters proudly wore a depiction of the yew. It wasn't just used as symbol in battle, however, but as a part of the battle too, in the bows and arrows of the King's bowmen.

Legend has it that this yew wood came from Inchlonraig, the most northerly island in Loch Lomond, opposite Luss. It is said that these trees were planted on the orders of Robert the Bruce to provide a source of wood for making longbows. Indeed, two venerable – but long since vanished – trees of large girth, measured in 1770, probably dated back to the 14th century, to Bruce's lifetime. Today the island is covered in hundreds of yew trees, and they and the rest of the woodland are now afforded protection within the Loch Lomond and the Trossachs National Park.

Doubt has always surrounded the authenticity of this being Robert the Bruce's yew tree. We know that the highly respected

Scottish botanist John Claudius Loudon (1783–1843) made the journey to Loch Lomond in 1837 to study the tree and recorded a height of 12 metres and took a trunk girth measurement of 3.96 metres at ground level. When measured in 1999 the girth was 6.10 metres –an increase of 2.14 metres in 162 years. Some say that taking into consideration the testing habitat conditions of a very exposed rocky site with typically low nutrient levels, which results in the slow growth of trees, the tree could have been at least 500 years old when Loudon visited. This means the tree was extant during Bruce's lifetime, but perhaps it was not of any great stature.

Counter to all this, when the pruned central stem was recently aged by counting its annual rings, it showed the tree to be little more than 350 years old. There remains the possibility that the name Robert the Bruce's Yew was transferred from a more ancient but long-gone tree, which grew close by. In 1811, records show that this much older yew tree had a massive girth of 8.5 metres with a crown in proportion, but by then was in a state of advanced decay.

Whatever the true identity of the tree at Stuc an T'Iobhairt, it is still much revered. Its height has become reduced as a result of heavy pruning, which took place in the 19th century, and it is heavily shaded by overhanging oak branches, but yews are very well adapted to dealing with shade. The bole is open on one side and shows the classic hollow trunk of veteran yew trees. Like all old trees, it is an important host to other forms of life, especially for the lower plants, such as mosses and fungi – it has become a habitat in its own right.

In recent years, the health of the tree has been evaluated using state-of-the-art equipment. Sonic tomography, or the use of sound waves to detect decay in trees, is a technology available to arboriculturists to create an image of the internal structure of a tree. The investigation revealed that about 58 per cent of the tree is decayed but 21 per cent is in good health and the rest of the tree is less degraded. But in the precarious world of ancient yew trees this state of health is nothing unusual – it is part and parcel of these trees getting old and the tree is likely to still remain for centuries to come.

Stevenson's Yew

This yew is perhaps one of Edinburgh's best-kept secrets and yet, with an age of over 400 years, it's possibly the city's oldest tree. Far more notable, though, are its links to the author Robert Louis Stevenson (1850–1894). Edinburgh has some remarkable hidden leafy locations, some of the most picturesque of which are associated with the city's only river – the Water of Leith. One such location is in the suburbs of the city, in what is still referred to as Colinton Village. Here, Stevenson's Yew stands in the grounds of the Old Manse, just behind St Cuthbert's Parish Church at the bottom of Dell Road, which runs down to a bend in the river. How fitting that today material from this tree is now conserved in a hedge which is only a stone's throw from Stevenson's birthplace at Howard Place, opposite the Royal Botanic Garden Edinburgh.

What a delightful part of the city this is, away from the hustle and bustle of everyday life and, in contrast, at peace with nature and all the joys that this brings. My last visit here was in early spring after many days of incessant rain and as a result the river was in full spate. The torrential waters did not prevent a pair of energetic kingfishers from making an early start with building their riverside nest. Glimpses were had of their iridescent blue plumage, flashing down the river as they searched for building material in sight of the great yew tree. For how long this tree has witnessed such events we're not sure; certainly it predates the construction of St Cuthbert's Church in 1650, for the tree was noted in Kirk Sessions minutes of 1630. For it to have been mentioned must mean that it was of a noteworthy size, but as for its exact age, we will probably never know.

As a young boy, Stevenson cherished his time spent on the swing which hung from the yew tree – today a new swing is hanging from the original brackets. Stevenson was a frequent visitor to the manse, home to his maternal grandfather Dr Lewis Balfour (1777–1860), who was the minister of St Cuthbert's Church. Ironically, in his later years, Stevenson distanced himself from Christianity and announced himself an atheist. Best known for his novels *Treasure Island*, *Kidnapped* and *The Strange Case of Dr Jekyll and Mr Hyde*, his early years spent in Colinton greatly influenced much of Stevenson's poetry, especially that relating to nature and, indeed, the yew tree.

In October 2013, Edinburgh's first outdoor statue of Stevenson was unveiled in the small garden outside St Cuthbert's Church. The bronze work depicts him as a boy sitting on a log with his Skye Terrier, Coolin. A year later in October 2014, 'A Walk with Robert Louis Stevenson' was opened. This poetry trail alludes to many of his works which refer to the yew tree. For example, 'To Minnie' from *A Child's Garden of Verses* (1885) reads: "A yew, which is one of the glories of the village. Under the circuit of its wide, black branches, it was always dark and cool, and there was a green scurf over all the trunk among which glistened the round, bright drops of resin." Again, the yew tree is featured in 'The Manse' from *Memories and Portraits* (1887):

> "Below the yew – it is still there –
> Our phantom voices haunt the air
> As we were still at play,
> And I can hear them call and say
> 'How far is it to Babylon?'"

Some 20 years ago, a very large café was constructed to the southern end of the church, adjacent to the manse. The Swing Café, as it is known, was inspired by Stevenson's poem about the swing in the yew tree on which he used to play. The location of the swing can be seen outside the Dell Room window of the café; in fact, the end of the café building is a matter of inches away from the 3.57-metre-diameter bole of the yew tree. I wonder if, in order to accommodate the building, the adjacent lateral branches had to be removed, or had these been cut off prior to the building being erected? Its celebrated status as one of Edinburgh's oldest trees, or indeed the link with one of Scotland's greatest authors, clearly had no sway in influencing the siting of the building, perhaps to be at a more respectful distance away from the magnificent yew tree. Some will say that the tree's notability prevented it from being removed altogether and it was its connection to Stevenson that meant it had to be preserved as a living memorial to him and his literary works.

According to the Charter for Woods, Trees and People, trees like Stevenson's Yew should be "listed a natural monument, along with their immediate environment, [and] deserve the same level of legal protection and financial management support as listed buildings and monuments". Notwithstanding the high level of disturbance, the Stevenson yew tree still remains strong and appears in very good condition – it is living proof of how extraordinarily resilient yew trees are and surely in this case, just how forgiving!

The 'Egg and Eggcup' Yews

Crathes Castle is a quintessential Scottish Tower House, built in the 16th century and tucked away on the north-east side of Aberdeenshire, close to Banchory. It was under the occupancy of the Burnett family, who lived in the castle for over 350 years, that the garden was developed, now renowned as one of the National Trust for Scotland's premier visitor attractions. An iconic feature of the garden, just below the castle at the entrance to the Croquet Lawn, is a pair of eccentric-looking topiary yews, affectionately referred to as the 'Egg and Eggcup'.

One has to admire the vision of early horticultural pioneers who had little or no previous knowledge to draw on, and indeed nor did they have the array of plant material that is available to us today. Crathes Castle is recognised for its remarkable yew hedges, the stature of which are largely unrivalled in Scottish gardens, or indeed throughout the wider UK. It is likely that the origin of the yew plants used for the hedges and topiaries were collected as seed and cuttings from local 'wild' stock. Indeed, to the observant eye, it is evident that the hedges are made up from a range of genetic material and not just a single clone, as there exists a great variation of colour from deep green to some of the young growth tinged golden yellow.

When I first saw the twin topiaries, they reminded me of two resting figures, their arms folded, and their faces covered by wide-brimmed sombreros. In her skilfully written and lavishly illustrated book *The Gardens and Landscape of Crathes Castle* (2019), Susan Bennett lets her imagination go into free-fall when describing these idiosyncratic trees: "There's something decidedly rebellious about the 'Egg and Eggcup' topiary yews that are so familiar to visitors to Crathes. A photograph of nearly 100 years ago shows the pair, then a mere two hundred years old, as perfectly symmetrical twin topiaries. Today they defy the gardeners' attempts to keep them in order. Despite the crisp August clipping, they lean and curve as if tipsy, like two old ladies, once prim and proper, who have lost their inhibitions having indulged in an extra sherry." Originally crafted into the shape of finials, I wonder what the gardeners of that era would think of them today? Horrified that the original design has not been respected or fascinated to see how their characters have 'evolved' into pieces of modern-day art? I hope the latter is the case.

With the help of dendrochronology, the age of the twin topiaries can now be verified as probably dating back to 1702. Cores were taken from the trunk of one of the trees in order to count the growth rings. Although this did not give an exact date of 1702, due to the rings of yew trees being very close together, or even missing in drought years, together with historical and archive records, it helped to confirm this date. It is not very often that we can give such an accurate age for yew trees, but in this case, we can be quite sure that the twin topiaries are around 320 years old.

Gone are the days when cutting the twin topiaries involved precariously leaning a ladder against their bulbous midribs and anchoring it to the ground using a garden fork. Nowadays, more sophisticated and less invasive equipment is being used, which gives safer access and prevents damage to the trees. Each year from the beginning of August, a mobile elevating work platform (MEWP) has now become a common sight in the grounds of Crathes Castle. The garden staff at Crathes can now apply their considerable skills in cutting the hedges and topiaries with agility and precision in order to get a very professional finish. More recently, other important changes have been made to consider the environment and the health of the users and visiting public. The Head Gardener, James Hannaford, proudly says, "our staff and visitors no longer have to tolerate the constant drone and the toxic fumes of a two-stroke engine running for weeks on end; we now use battery-powered hedge cutters".

John Knox's Yew

This solitary tree stands on the lawn close to Finlaystone House with a commanding view over the Firth of Clyde at Landbank in Renfrewshire. It is of no great stature for a reputed age of between 500 and 600 years old, but its claim to fame is that in the 16th century John Knox preached beneath its canopy. In 1900 the tree's notability influenced the owner of Finlaystone House not to fell the tree, but rather move it, as the canopy was casting too much shade on the principal rooms of the house.

Perhaps this is one of the most underwhelming old yew trees I have encountered in my journey throughout Britain and Ireland in search of heritage trees, and yet its reputed historical link perhaps makes up for it. Although its origins are uncertain, it is said to have been planted by John Knox himself in the mid-16th century. However, there are also observations that indicate the tree was already of substantial size during his lifetime (c. 1514–1572) and it is one of the many trees under which he preached. It is said that he performed

the first ever Protestant Reformed communion service under the
yew in 1556 for Alexander Cunningham, the Earl of Glencairn,
and his family. The Earl was said to be an outspoken supporter
of Reformation. It is thought that Knox chose outdoor preaching
because churches were closing their doors to him and alternative
venues were required to pursue his campaign of Reformation.
Certainly, for personal safety reasons, being outside was better than
the possibility of being trapped in a building if anyone untoward
came in search of the unpopular religious reformer.

The modest-sized yew tree forks into two stems at ground level with
girths of 2.28 and 1.8 metres. The dense canopy is somewhat lop-
sided and if you are a geomorphologist, it is redolent of a postglacial
geological formation known as a *roche moutonnée*, literally the profile of
a grazing sheep. Sadly, the west face of the crown has started to die
back due to exposure to harsh prevailing winds. The tree also leans
and has been supported by an iron prop, but essentially, considering
its exposed position, it remains in good condition.

Perhaps its small stature for its age is because, as stated, in 1900
the tree was moved 30 metres to the south of the house. This was
part of a major refurbishment of the house in which it was
decided that the tree was blocking too much light. At great expense
George Jardine Kidston, a very wealthy Clyde shipping magnate,
employed a company from the USA to undertake the ambitious
task of relocating the tree. They carefully excavated the root ball
and placed a timber sled underneath it that was glided along
timber runners lining the base of a specially prepared trench which
terminated at the new planting position.

This extremely skilled operation was not a common practice of
the day, certainly not involving established yew trees, therefore
one should be full of admiration for the success of this ambitious

undertaking. In the 1850s a similar plan to move a yew tree was deemed to be too risky when the Prussian king, Frederick William IV wanted to rescue a yew tree from the extension of a government building. With the conclusion that it was too risky, instead the building plans were changed and the yew tree was left alone. However, in 1907 an English consultant helped with a spectacular relocation of a mature yew tree in the Berlin Botanical Garden. The 12-metre-tall tree in question was over 200 years old and weighed a staggering 42.5 tons. The four-metre-square root system was contained in a wooden box and the tree was moved 3.5 kilometres on a system of rollers, and pulled to its new location by two steamrollers. Perhaps lessons learnt from moving the John Knox tree helped when planning to relocate this tree.

The Auld Yew of Loudoun

Two very old yew trees, growing close to the south wall of
Loudoun Castle, are remarkable not so much for their
stature but for the fact that they survived the great fire of
1941, which completely gutted the castle. Today, the forlorn and
ruinous building stands at the end of a long driveway, backed by
mature woodland and enlivened by two dark green, dome-shaped
yew trees, one of which is said to be 800 years old. Situated in
Ayrshire, about one mile north-east of the old mill town of Galston,
just north of the River Irvine, Loudoun Castle has witnessed many
eventful and disturbing periods, one of which has happened in
recent years. When I first learnt of Loudoun Castle and its famous
yew trees, I immediately thought of a connection with the famous
Scottish botanist and garden designer John Claudius Loudon
but alas none exists. Loudoun Castle was originally built in the
15th century as a four- storey keep, and became the home of
Flora Mure Campbell, Countess of Loudoun and Marchioness

of Hastings (1780–1840). Constructed over a period of seven years around the existing keep, from 1804 to 1811, it eventually became known as the Windsor of Scotland. Certainly, it was a palatial building, comprising 90 rooms and including a 10,000-volume library, but alas, the final, ambitious structure was never completed as the family were unable to raise the necessary finances.

The castle was built within a few metres of the two yew trees, which look out onto the rose garden. The largest tree (which is male), standing to the left as one views the castle from the meadow below, is known as 'The Auld Yew of Loudoun'. Sadly, much of the upper canopy on the castle side of the tree has been lost – probably this happened during the construction of the castle. Incredibly, it appears to have escaped any lasting damage from this, or from the inferno that destroyed the fabric of the castle. It was during the Second World War, on 1st December 1941, when the castle was being used to accommodate Belgian troops, that the fire was accidentally started on the first floor of the library. Despite these events 'The Auld Yew of Loudoun' and its smaller neighbouring female tree are still in good health.

The Auld Yew is one of Scotland's famous trysting trees – it was there when the Earl of Loudoun and his close colleagues met to discuss drafts of the Treaty of Union with England in 1603. The castle also has links with famous Scottish heroes, one of whom is William Wallace. In fact, a treasured family possession was one of his swords, which hung on the east wall of the entrance hall of the castle until it was sold at auction in 1930. Wallace's name has long been linked to the area after he and his men dramatically defeated the English in a fierce onslaught at Loudoun Hill in 1297.

There is little doubt that 'The Auld Yew of Loudoun' has seen much turmoil and change during its long life. This includes happenings in more recent times, when the castle became the centrepiece of a theme park and opened as such in 1995 attracting over 200,000 visitors a year. However, 2010 saw the closure of the park due in part to a tragic accident but also for financial reasons.

Today the castle still stands, a shadow of its former self, but steadfast and cheek by jowl with the two faithful yew trees on its southern flank. Both trees are protected by a very high and impenetrable metal fence – at last, yew trees being afforded the protection they deserve! The fence, it transpires, is there to prevent the public from accessing the unsafe structure of the castle rather than for the trees. However, having met the owner of the Loudoun estate, he assures me that in the plans to restore and repurpose the castle to become a country house, the yew trees will be protected from any further intrusion.

The Traquair Yew

Hidden away in the woodlands of Traquair House, nestled in the rolling countryside of the Scottish Borders, is a mysterious circle of four yew trees. These old and gnarled trees sit on the floodplain of the Quair Water, a tributary of the River Tweed. Whether or not they are a remnant of the ancient royal hunting forest that once clothed the surrounding hills is a source of much speculation.

From a distance, the yew trees are not a prominent feature in the landscape. In fact, at first, it is difficult to identify the location, their stature dwarfed and shrouded by the canopy of towering examples of Douglas fir, Scots pine and lime trees. These relatively fast-growing trees, which line the banks of the Quair Water, may well be taller, but are only half the age of the yews. One can access the yews by following a heavily shaded trail itself dominated by yew trees, known as Lady Louisa's Walk, which leads to the river. The walk is named after Lady Louisa Stuart, sister of the 9th Earl of Traquair, who is said to haunt the grounds even to this day. The circle of four trees is opposite a part of the river known as the Ladies' Bathing Pool, where perhaps the ladies of the house would once have washed and relaxed.

The trees stand in the four corners of a square; whether this is the result of deliberate planting or accident is not known, but perhaps we should simply admire these contorted trees as a wonderful quirk of nature. Their appearance is graphically described by Rodger et al. in *Heritage Trees of Scotland* (2003), who say, "Their hunched and twisted limbs give the impression of four old men bent over in discussion, and the dark inner cavern formed by their dense foliage is eerily atmospheric". Just how many of the long-reaching branches have intertwined with those of neighbouring trees is notable and these have clearly become united (grafted). The four trees stand close to the river,

where a small, raised bank is frequently breached after heavy rainfall. Most conifer species, including the yews, resent prolonged periods of waterlogged soils, but as long as this flooding is seasonal and not prolonged, then no lasting damage will be caused to the trees.

Today this quartet of trees has created a stage for ceremonies such as weddings, poetry readings and prayers. They are even used as a setting for promenade plays, the Fairy Queen's arbour and a place where Macbeth's witches stir their cauldron. The location also hosts more mystical events, the yew being one of the most important trees in nature worship, thought to have magical and metaphysical properties. It is not unusual to hear the monotonous sound of Shamanic Drumming resonating from within the site of the four trees. Led by a local Shaman, faithful followers are taken on a Shamanic Journey to help them connect with the spirit of the yew tree in order to discover its magical powers, thought to help heal ancestral wounds.

Traquair House is built in the style of a fortified mansion and pre-dates the Scottish Baronial style of architecture. It became a royal administrative centre and, because it was used as a royal hunting lodge to Ettrick Forest, it was visited by 27 Scottish Kings and Queens, including the enigmatic Mary Queen of Scots, in 1566. The building dates back to 1107 and has been the home of the Stuart family since 1491, making it one of the oldest continually inhabited buildings in Scotland. The history of the house is well established, but what is not as certain is the age of the four yew trees. Commonly cited as being 1,000 years old or more, a more realistic estimate is of at least 400 years. The natural distribution of yew is thought to be restricted to southern Scotland, but there is little evidence of remnant woodlands surviving to the present day. Could these four yew trees once have been part of this natural distribution, which formed part of the Ettrick Forest? Perhaps we will never know.

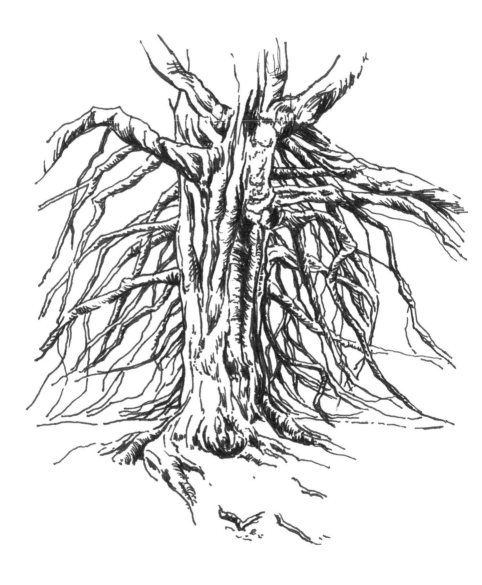

The Whittingehame Yew

My first visit to the Whittingehame Yew was in the company of Ulrich Loening and his wife Francesca, who travelled the short distance from their home just a few metres from the famous Ormiston Yew. It had been many years since their last visit and they wanted to reconnect with this remarkable tree. The visit was also part of a wider celebration for Ulrich, who had just become a nonagenarian and was about to mark 50 years since he established the Centre for Human Ecology at the University of Edinburgh.

It is often the case that old yew trees present a modest canopy, low and spreading, with no obvious emergent central canopy. While the Whittingehame Yew is indeed low and spreading, it is storied with a prominent, rising central canopy that is much loftier than trees with a similar growth habit. Viewed from the nearby Whittingehame Tower (what remains of Whittingehame Castle), one gets a sense of its symmetry, formed by the branches radiating from the central tree.

If it were not for the browsing deer that keep in check the upswept outer curtain of growth, the tree would slowly continue encroaching into the surrounding area, engulfing everything in its midst. These vast expanding trees often have a hidden 'doorway' that gives access through a curtain of foliage opening up into the canopy and finally to the main trunk. At first the Whittingehame Yew has no obvious entry point, until you arrive to the rear of the tree: down a gentle slope there is a tell-tale sign, a worn grass path leading to what looks like the entrance to an opencast mineshaft.

Until recently, the only access to this tree was to crouch low, as if you were entering a small tent. However, the access has now been

modified by using a series of overhead wooden supports to allow
a more comfortable walk in. The passageway leads up a 25-metre
slope, through a cascade of falling branches into a large open
chamber to the main trunk. Once inside, one is surrounded by
a dense entanglement of serpent-like branches, which on reaching
the ground have layered, some sending up robust new trees.
What is surprising for the size of the tree, is that the main trunk
is a relatively modest 3.30 metres when measured one metre from
ground level.

Unlike the Ormiston Yew, which is of similar form, there is no
obvious hollowing, which is unusual for a tree of this stature.
The size of the trunk suggests an age of only 300–350 years.

However, legend has it that the tree was of note in 1566, when the then-resident of Whittingehame Castle, Lord Morton, together with his fellow noblemen, hatched a plot under its canopy to murder Lord Darnley, the king consort to Mary Queen of Scots. Apparently, when Arthur Balfour of Whittingehame (Prime Minister from 1902 to 1905) was asked if the story of the plot was true, he replied that "it had more historical plausibility about it than many legends".

The Twyford Yew

The Taxal Yew

The Borrowdale Yews

The Stow-on-the-World Yews

The Much Marcle Yew

The Darwin Yews

The Ankerwycke Yew

The Muncaster Yew

The Crowhurst Yews

The Selborne Yew

The Martindale Yew

The Bampton Church Yews

The Ashbrittle Yew

England

The native yew woodlands of England are most common in the south of the country on the chalk downs, where they often occur with beech, box, and juniper. Fine examples of yew woodland can also be found on limestone hills in County Durham and Cumbria. The Yew Conservation Hedge contains trees from the famous Kingley Vale forest, West Sussex and from the scarcely known, discreet site at Woody Bay on the coast of North Devon. Yew trees form a prominent component of designed landscapes in England, with the majority of older heritage trees occurring in churchyards. With over 3,000 trees to choose from, 13 were selected for planting in the Hedge. Most are from famous churchyard trees, but the selection also includes trees associated with two very famous people – the poet William Wordsworth and the naturalist Charles Darwin.

NATIVE YEWS

The Kingley Vale Yews

The mention of UK native yews invariably brings to mind Kingley Vale, such is the renown of this yew woodland. It is said to be one of Europe's most impressive yew forests. The 500- year-old yew trees clothe the chalk grassland slopes of the South Downs near to Chichester in West Sussex. Kingley Vale is also synonymous with Sir Arthur Tansley (1871–1955), widely recognised as 'the founding father of British ecology', who cherished Kingley Vale. He ensured that this unique habitat was protected when, n 1952, it became one of the first National Nature Reserves to be acquired by the Nature Conservancy, of which he was the first Chair.

Today this is one of 4,000 Sites of Special Scientific Interest in England and is managed by Natural England and West Dean Estate. In his captivating book *The Great Yew Forest*, Richard Williamson gives witness to his first visit to Kingley Vale in 1963 as follows: "These slopes were covered with dense yew forests, crown upon crown touching and leaving no opening, a canopy of dark green. Thus, they formed an amphitheatre, and in the pit of this I felt small – not insignificant but rather, out of place… Deeper into the wood I went and came upon some ancient trees whose boughs drooped around them and touched the ground… One monster had grown such a long bough that this had broken near the trunk and now hung with a splintered gape like a crocodile's mouth."

The scene is much the same today, a wilderness of over 200 hectares, steeped in history. It is said that Kingley Vale was originally planted as a memorial for a battle fought between the Anglo-Saxons and the Vikings in 850 CE, and folklore has it that the woodlands were once used as a secret meeting place for Druids over 2,000 years ago. The yews also witnessed a very noisy and disturbing time during both the First and Second World Wars when the Vale was used as a rifle range.

In November 2007, I was part of a group, which included Tom Christian and Dan Luscombe, Curator of the Bedgebury National Pinetum in Kent, who made collections from 12 trees, which are now represented in the Hedge by 66 new trees.

The Lynton Yews

In contrast to the well-known Kingley Vale forest, the yews along the rugged Exmoor coast of North Devon, close to the picturesque town of Lynton, are scarcely known. The majority grow on steep, inaccessible rocky slopes between West Woody Bay and Hollow Coombes; however, it is thought that the full extent of the population stretches further, for seven kilometres between Lee Abbey and Trentishoe. The seed collections here were made in November 2011, by one of the Royal Botanic Garden Edinburgh's arboriculturists, William Hinchliffe, along with Kester Webb and botanist Dr David Aplin. Kester Webb and his wife Elizabeth have spent 50 years exploring this remote coastline and have taken a great interest in the yew population.

This stretch of coast has the highest sea cliffs in southern England and the world's second largest tidal range; hence many parts of the coast are difficult to access. Most of the yews grow as low, mound-like shrubs on steep rocky slopes, which require a rope and harness to access. William's fieldwork led him to believe that these cliffs are an important refuge for trees and act as a vital seed source for other nearby woodland habitats. The yews have been shaped into low shrubs at the behest of strong coastal winds and continuous browsing by deer and feral goats, but there is protection as the area has been designated a Site of Special Scientific Interest. What is of great concern is the instability of the steep cliffs, which could lead to landslips and severe erosion that would be of great detriment to the yew population. Some yews grow on sessile oak-dominated woodland edges where they are afforded some protection from wind-pruning, and here they can attain heights of up to four metres tall.

William, who has led a small team of horticulturists in the planting of the Yew Conservation Hedge, is excited to see 46 trees from the North Devon population established within it.

HERITAGE YEWS

The Ankerwycke Yew

Quietly standing on the floodplain of the River Thames, close to Runnymede in Berkshire, is one of Britain's most famous trees. Some have even said it is the most important tree in the English-speaking world, as it is thought to be the site of the signing of *Magna Carta*, a bill of rights, which has become a powerful symbol of liberty around the world. This enigmatic tree of colossal proportions is thought to have an age of 1,400 years, but some give estimates of up to 2,500 years old. Whatever the truth, it is clear that the Ankerwycke Yew is of great national and international importance, and as such in 1998 it was taken into protection by the National Trust.

The yew is part of a woodland community on Ankerwycke Island that is bounded by the River Thames and a small meandering moat. The island is a component of a natural meadow system that is subject to seasonal flooding. The course of the river has changed over the last millennium, partly due to forces of nature, but also from artificial widening for navigational purposes. Within a short distance of the tree stands St Mary's Priory, built in 1160 and founded by the Benedictine nuns. However, unlike the yew tree, it has not survived the test of time – following the dissolution of the monasteries it has gradually fallen into disrepair and today only survives as a crumbling shell.

Like all yews, the Ankerwycke tree is a master of longevity, for it has an extraordinary armament to draw on for survival. Many centuries ago the trunk started to decay due to the presence of wood-rotting fungi, though this intrusion did not weaken the tree. Instead, the resulting thinner outer wall of the trunk has given a greater degree of strength.

The agent was most likely to have been 'chicken of the woods' – this bracket fungus is globular in shape and sulphur-coloured, but as it matures becomes fan-like and fades to pale yellow. It is called chicken of the woods because it has the texture and the taste of chicken; hence the young fruiting bodies are highly prized by foragers.

However, be warned, some say that if harvested from a yew tree, it will have absorbed some of the poisons from the tree and could therefore be dangerous to eat. Mycologists refute this claim and say that it is more likely that twigs and needles have become incorporated into the rapidly growing fungus and that these have been missed during the cleaning and cooking process – although forager and chef Mark Williams states: "Given that 50 grams of yew needles is estimated as a potentially lethal dose for an adult, you'd need to be pretty shoddy with your cleaning to kill yourself!"

Apparently the meadow of Runnymede, the site of this famous tree, is where Anglo-Saxons used to hold council about the welfare of the state. Indeed, the name Runnymede is derived from the Anglo-Saxon 'runeig' meaning regular meeting and 'mede' for meadow. The location cited for the signing of Magna Carta on 15th June 1215 is 'Ronimed. Inter Widlesoram et Stanes' – between Windsor and Staines. Historians agree that the meadow of Runnymede was the general location for the famous event, although some have said that there is no direct evidence that signing took place under the Ankerwycke Yew.

On 15th June 1992, 777 years after Magna Carta was signed, a group of conservationists met at the tree, with the exuberant environmental campaigner David Bellamy, to make an oath – a green Magna Carta. The oath was to protect life on Earth and included ten pledges for protecting all forms of life, granting them rights, and to allow them to "live and complete their cycles of life as ordained by nature".

Today the great Ankerwycke Yew continues to grow old quietly and gracefully while the age debate persists. A tree-ring analysis was carried out on a branch that fell from the tree during the winter of 1989/90, which proved to be 317 years old. This information will be crucial when recalculating the age of the tree, but for this to happen further tree-ring analysis of the main trunk will be needed. Until this happens the consensus of opinion is that there is little doubt the tree was fully grown at the time of the signing of Magna Carta and predates St Mary's Priory. Together with a girth measurement of 7.88 metres, an age of at least 1,400 years is confidently given for the Ankerwycke Yew.

The Ashbrittle Yew

The route to this famous old yew tree is through a series of meandering lanes within the heart of the English countryside, that lead to the small and ancient hilltop village of Ashbrittle in Somerset. Standing just south-east of St John the Baptist Church, its huge canopy dominates the churchyard and overlooks the River Tone. There are some wild and fanciful claims of its age ranging from 3,000 to 4,000 years – it is a very old tree, but perhaps not as old as these dates claim. However, this is one of 50 'Great British Trees' chosen to celebrate the Queen's Golden Jubilee in 2002.

The plaque next to the tree states that the yew is over 3,000 years old and goes on to say, "This tree was mature when Stonehenge was in use, predating the church by over 2,000 years. Its origin is obscure but may have been planted to mark a holy place, or remains from a nearby battle." Even though the origins of the village of Ashbrittle predate historical records, we do know that a church was built here from 1251. It is highly likely though that this location would have been attractive to human habitation due to the presence of underground springs. During the Victorian restoration of the church, in about 1874, a spring was discovered directly under the altar, which suggests a sacred site of early origin. Even a geophysical survey, carried out at the church in 2004, failed to provide conclusive evidence for the earliest phases of the site.

The yew tree was planted on what is thought to be a barrow, (sometimes referred to as a tumulus), which is an ancient burial place covered with a large mound of earth. This is about 1.5 metres high by 15 metres across. Although there is no archaeological

evidence, it is said to be of Bronze Age construction. In his essay on the Ashbrittle Yew (2020), Tim Hills, from The Ancient Yew Group, has recorded many stories relating to the barrow, although none have been verified. These stories include "battles fought in the area with Roman soldiers, and the heads of defeated warriors carried victoriously back to the site and buried on the mound". He continues, "some say a pre-Roman chief is buried here; others that the church was built on a druid circle, with red-stained bones found near the mound, testifying to a common pagan practice".

This male tree has a vast canopy and typically its branches skirt the ground on all sides. It comprises a central stem, which does not appear to be hollow, encircled by six others, which lean outwards; these are up to 4.9 metres in girth. The general opinion is that these stems are fragments of a former larger single-stemmed tree. In 2015, local concerns reported a decline in the health of the tree, with much of the foliage turning yellow and an unusual amount of leaf loss. However, expert opinion was of the view that this was merely a normal phase that the tree was going through.

The plaque that stands in front of the tree was installed as a local celebration. Part of the inscription says: "Generations of local people have cherished this tree, one of the oldest living things in Britain". Importantly, it also implores visitors to respect the tree and not to climb its branches. The inscription ends with a Wordsworth poem written in 1813 about the Lorton Yew in northern England. His words also aptly apply to the Ashbrittle tree.

> "Of vast circumference and gloom profound
> This solitary Tree! a living thing
> Produced too slowly ever to decay;
> Of form and aspect too magnificent
> To be destroyed."

The Bampton Church Yews

St Michael's Church lies at the heart of the delightful Devonshire town of Bampton, which sits in a beautiful sheltered wooded valley. This historic Charter Town in mid-Devon is close to the Somerset border, on the edge of the Exmoor National Park. Yews are a dominant feature in the churchyard; certainly, it is difficult to miss the two larger trees – their trunks are entirely encased in a stone surround. It is these trees that were selected for inclusion in the Yew Conservation Hedge.

Interestingly, my overnight stay there was at the Swan Hotel in Bampton, which is one of the oldest buildings in the town, built in 1450 to accommodate the stonemasons who worked on the construction of St Michael's Church. It is to the south of the church (within a few metres) where the two yew trees grow; one is in front of the south porch while the other stands in a direct line from it, about 12 metres away, opposite the far end of the nave.

There is some conflicting information regarding the ages of these two trees. Caroline Seaward in her publication, *The Book of Bampton* (2003), gives remarkably precise planting dates of between 1483 and 1485, which makes them over 530 years old. It is not clear where this information originated. The Ancient Yew Group reports the male tree opposite the south porch to be 'Ancient', so 800 years or more old and with a girth measurement of at least seven metres. This tree has a girth measurement of 8.8 metres, but it is not known how this measurement was obtained, considering the tree is encased in stone. For the second tree, which is female, a category of 'Veteran' is given, 500 years or more old with a girth of at least 4.9 metres – the most recent measurement is 5.7 metres (at 2.4 metres from the ground). Further confusion arises from a caption to an image in *The Book of Bampton* of the tree opposite the south porch of the church. It states that in 1979 half of its canopy was destroyed and goes on to say "the remainder removed for safety reasons" – but this cannot be the case as the tree still thrives today.

Exactly when it was decided to cover the trunks of the yew trees in stone is not known, but the reason is clear – to protect livestock, such as cows and sheep, from grazing on the poisonous foliage. Swanton, writing in his booklet *The Yew Trees of England* in 1958, quotes a Leslie Giltrow as saying of these trees, "Ancient yews with some stone seats around them, and the crevices of the trees filled with masonry". Subsequently, when the surrounds were rebuilt, the cost of incorporating seating was considered too expensive. However, in the recent reconstruction of the stone jacket of one of the trees, the seating has been reinstated.

Clearly at one time the churchyard of St Michael's was not
enclosed by a continuous hedge or wall, which meant that livestock
could freely wander into the churchyard to graze. The fact that

the livestock market was once sited next to the church (now with residential houses on a site called Market Close), probably meant that some of the local sheep and cattle were driven through the churchyard to the market. It is important to remember that all parts of the yew are highly toxic, except for the red aril that surrounds the seed, and all livestock can be affected. The reason for this toxicity is the presence of the alkaloid taxine. Ingested yew damages the nervous system and the liver, but its most severe effect is on the cardiac muscles, resulting in heart failure and death. As mentioned earlier, deer have been able to build up immunity to the toxic effects of yew, hence many unprotected heritage yew trees have a characteristic browse line.

The Borrowdale Yews

Immortalized by the Romantic poet William Wordsworth (1770–1850) in his poem *Yew-Trees*, this small group of yew trees in the remote valley of Borrowdale in the Lake District is amongst the most famous in the British Isles. His poem starts by celebrating the Cumbrian yew of Lorton Vale and makes comparisons with the four trees in Borrowdale:

"… But worthier still of note
Are those fraternal Four of Borrowdale,
Joined in one solemn and capacious grove;
Huge trunks! – and each particular trunk a growth
Of intertwisted fibres serpentine
Up-coiling, and inveterately convolved…"

For all its beauty and apparent tranquillity, the Lake District is also known for its extreme weather events, and the rugged and exposed Borrowdale Valley is no exception. Sadly, one of the four trees was uprooted by a ferocious storm in 1866, and subsequent storms have reshaped the canopies of the remaining three trees, one of which, alas, was severely damaged by another powerful storm in 2005. Today the three female trees cling to the craggy slopes as shadows of their former selves; even so they are still much revered. The largest of this trio was chosen as one of the 50 'Great British Trees' to celebrate the Queen's Golden Jubilee. Its canopy, which was cruelly reduced by 50 per cent in a recent gale, is supported by a robust hollow trunk with a girth of about 7.5 metres.

The local area has been protected by the National Trust since 1944, although it is not just the yews of Borrowdale being protected but unique remnants of Atlantic Oak Woodlands that were once widespread, covering the north-western seaboard of Europe, from Scotland to northern Spain and Portugal. Amongst the mosaic of oak-, ash- and hazel-covered hillsides, native yew is a rare sight; indeed there is much discussion concerning the origins of the three ancient yew trees, as some consider them to be planted.

Archaeological studies of this valley, especially of areas close to the yew trees, have revealed some fascinating details concerning the extent of human activity, some dating back to the 1400s. The woodlands have been managed for many centuries, with pollarding a common practice for providing wood for use in crafting tool handles and as a source of firewood. The most notable activity in the Borrowdale Valley, especially in the vicinity of the yew trees, has been mining for graphite. The mine here was the only graphite mine in the UK, and in fact contained the only substantial deposit of graphite ever found in a solid form anywhere in the world.

Near to the old yew trees there was once a guardhouse; so valuable was the graphite that labourers were watched carefully to prevent its theft. Further evidence of mining can be seen in the remains of a nearby saw pit, which was once used to produce sawn timber for use in the mines. When graphite was first discovered in the 16th century it was used for marking sheep and later as a medicine, but its main uses have been as an industrial lubricant and in pencils.

There is speculation that what appears to be the remains of stone terracing, upon which the trees grow, was once a place of ritual or worship, giving further evidence that these trees were once planted purposely.

Today many questions remain about these iconic trees, especially those relating to their age and if they are related to each other. One of the group is thought to be about 1,000 years old, but following a ferocious storm in 1998, when a limb was torn from the tree, University of Newcastle dendrochronologists set about the task of gaining a more accurate age. With the use of a scanning electron microscope, they counted the growth rings, which incredibly revealed an age of 1,500 years – but surely the tree will be older as this count was taken from a limb and not from the main trunk! As a result of recent advances in DNA fingerprinting, we now know that two of the trees are the same clone, while the third tree is genetically distinct. It is thought that the two related trees are the result of a branch collapsing to the ground and rooting, hence a secondary branch has formed and grown into what appears to be a separate tree.

In 2012, Toby Hindson, founder member of The Ancient Yew Group, described the small grove of trees at the head of the Borrowdale Valley as a "scene of ruin and regeneration". For at least 1,500 years these stunted and gnarled structures have literally weathered every storm that has come their way, but still they manage to hold their own and regrow from their battered crowns. Such is their resistance to the vagaries of the ferocious weather systems of the Lake District, they will probably still fascinate and enchant visitors for another 1,500 years or more to come.

The Crowhurst Yew

The churchyard of St George's Church in Crowhurst village, East Sussex, is the location of an ancient yew tree, thought to predate the arrival of William the Conqueror. This magnificent yew grows to the south of the churchyard adjacent to a path leading to the church. It is said to have stood here for at least 1,300 years, having been planted in about 700 AD. Sometimes referred to as the 1066 Yew, it has very strong links to both William the Conqueror and the Anglo-Saxon King Harold. As part of the 950th anniversary of the Battle of Hastings commemorations in 2016, a plaque was placed on the railings surrounding the tree by the Lord Lieutenant of East Sussex. The text reads: "1066–2016. This ancient yew was here in 1066 when King Harold owned the

Manor of Crowhurst. In this 950th anniversary year of the Battle of Hastings we remember his close links to this part of Sussex."

Incredibly, this old yew has a doppelganger at St George's Parish Church at Crowhurst in Surrey, and as a result the two trees have sometimes been confused. This confusion over names, however, is where their similarities end, even though both have a wide opening to the main trunk. The name Crowhurst comes from the Anglo-Saxon 'Crohha hyrst' meaning muddy hill. Apparently, King Offa of Mercia gave the Bishop of Selsey eight hides, and in exchange the Bishop built a church for the community. Being next to the magnificent tower of this ancient church, which dominates the skyline, is such a dramatic setting for this distinctive yew tree, which is itself full of character. Some say the twisted bark depicts the face of an old man sticking his tongue out! Perhaps it should be considered that of an old woman, because this tree is female, sporting bright scarlet fruits in the autumn.

Fascination with this tree dates back to 1680 when John Aubrey, a 17th-century archaeologist, took the first measurements; he recorded a height of just over ten metres and a girth of 8.3 metres. Together with subsequent girth measurements, this has helped to ascertain the growth rate over a period of 332 years, which has given a calculation of 2.6 millimetres per year. Today, the height is 12 metres with a girth of 9.08 metres, but the main trunk is continuing to open up, which will eventually result in it separating into two distinctive fragments. As far back as the mid-1800s there is mention of the wide opening increasing in size due to "a falling away of a large portion of the tree on the south side". Today this leaning portion of the tree is almost touching the protective railings. If its downward movement is unhindered it will fall to the ground and, if still attached to the mother tree, will continue the next stage in its extraordinary life.

The tree was first protected by an iron railing in 1907, since when a funding campaign has been launched for its further protection. At one time iron bands were placed around the parting trunk, along with branch cabling, chains and props to prevent the branches from falling to the ground. Every conceivable form of protection has been employed, even metal hawsers, thick cables more traditionally used for mooring or towing ships, which were used to replace the iron bands. All of this has been carried out with the intention of improving the health of the tree and prolonging its life. Ironically, this well-intentioned arboricultural maintenance is preventing the tree from laying its branches on the ground to rest – the well-known strategy used by 'walking' yew trees to support their ageing limbs and ensure longevity. However, harnessing such encroachment when space is at a premium is fully understandable – sadly, not every yew tree can be allowed to sprawl into fantastical, sculptural shapes and reach their full magnificent potential.

St George's churchyard has two other impressive yew trees, both of which are also female. They are thought to have been planted by Sir John Pelham, the constable of nearby Pevensey Castle, in the 15th century, which, at about 600 years old, makes them less than half the age of the celebrated Crowhurst Yew.

The Darwin Yews

The Yew Conservation Hedge would not be complete without a link to one of the most famous people in history, Charles Darwin (1809–1882), who of course wrote the ground-breaking work *On the Origin of Species by Means of Natural Selection* (1859). For the Royal Botanic Garden Edinburgh, as a world-leading scientific institution, it is appropriate to have this link as few other individuals have had so much influence on modern scientific thinking as the polymath Charles Darwin. There were two appropriate options when it came to selecting yew trees for the Hedge with a link to the 'father of evolution'. Firstly the ancient tree that stands in the churchyard of St Mary's Church in the small village of Downe, Greater London, which was the Parish Church that Darwin attended and where several members of his family are buried. Or secondly the two trees at the nearby Down House, Darwin's last family home. The latter were chosen.

It is interesting to note that Darwin had a connection with the city of Edinburgh because in 1825, at the tender age of 16, he followed in his father and uncle's footsteps and attended the University of Edinburgh to read medicine. However, after two years he dropped out and went to Cambridge to study theology. Crucially, it was during his time in Scotland that he became exposed to theories of evolution, and this greatly influenced Darwin's views later in his professional life.

Down House, in Kent, is less than a kilometre away from the small village of Downe, which was spelt as Down when Darwin moved to his house in 1842. It was in the 1940s that the name was changed to Downe, apparently to avoid any possible confusion with County Down in Northern Ireland. During his time at the house with his wife Emma, the couple invested a lot of time in developing the house and garden, the latter of which was used by Charles as an open-air laboratory. The two yew trees in front of Down House are not especially statuesque or of any great age, but over a period of 40 years they witnessed the daily lives of this very famous family. The yews were an important focal point under which the family would sit and relax, and the children, of which there were ten, used to spend much of their time swinging between the two trees.

The Martindale Yew

I f faced with the difficult decision of choosing a favourite heritage yew, then the Martindale tree would most certainly feature in my top five. It is not just its enormity (with a canopy diameter of over 18 metres), and its extraordinary juxtaposition with the Church of St Martin's, but also its remote setting with spectacular views across one of the most picturesque parts of the Lake District that makes this such a remarkable and cherished tree.

The exciting journey to Martindale Church starts by taking the road that snakes along the eastern margins of Ullswater from Pooley Bridge, past the hamlet of Howtown almost to the end of the valley. From here an open mountain road winds its way up through several hairpin bends to the church of St Peter at Martindale House. It is then a short distance from here, down a hill, that the Old Church of St Martin's, and the yew tree, first come into view.

Inseparable from the simple single-chamber, dry stone Cumbrian church, the yew tree stands high up in the Martindale Valley with a commanding view across the rugged and largely treeless landscape of the Lake District National Park. This extraordinary tree, with its low spreading branches contained in a disproportionally small churchyard, is like a cuckoo in a nest – ever increasing in size and constantly competing for space with the church. If the right of occupancy were ever contested then perhaps the yew tree would be the clear winner; it almost certainly predates the church. Its age is estimated to be between 700 and 2,000 years; growth measurements carried out by the Ancient Tree Group suggest the lower end of this range. Certainly, 1,300 years is the age frequently cited in literature on yew trees.

The church itself is dedicated to St Martin of Tours, reputedly a Roman soldier who later converted to the Christian faith. Certainly, the first Christians will have carefully chosen this site for building a church because of the presence of a yew tree, representing a site that is already sacred. In its early days, and up until the dissolution of the monasteries in 1536, St Martin's was served by the monks of the parish of Barton. The first reference to this site being used as a place of worship is unknown, but there are references stating that a chapel was already in existence in 1220. However, the present building was erected towards the end of the 16th century, since when there have been successive restorations, the last in 1882, when the roof was replaced following violent storms. Perhaps the position of the church gives a degree of protection to the yew tree, and acts as a first line of defence against any incoming storms. Unlike the church building, yew trees will self-repair any damage caused by strong winds – they are masters of branch replenishment.

The Martindale Yew consists of two trunks that are joined low down near the base. One of the trunks is a hollow shell 'eaten out' by fungal rot, and has developed numerous branches, one of which dips down to the ground. Such grounded branches become embedded in the soil, and help to anchor the tree; in time they will produce new shoots – and so this tree continues its slow encroachment of the churchyard. The second trunk, closest to the church, has a small hollow, and one of its many branches also dips to the ground. It is from this second trunk that cuttings for the Yew Conservation Hedge were selected because it is covered with adventitious twiggy growth, which is ideal material for yew cuttings.

Beneath the tree is a tomb where Richard Birkett, the first priest of St Martin's, is interred. Birkett became the church's first resident priest; he served until his death on Christmas Day in 1699 at the age of 95, after a ministry of almost 67 years. His well-preserved epitaph states he left a sum of £100 "towards the better maintenance of a godly, sober and religious Minister at Martindale Chapell".

Today the church is rarely used save for special summer events as there is no electricity to heat the building. However, the yew tree, in all its magnificence, is a popular visitor attraction to those who enjoy the adventure down the single-track road to the head of the spectacular Martindale Valley.

The Much Marcle Yew

The ancient yew tree in the tiny Herefordshire village of Much Marcle dominates the churchyard of St Bartholomew's Church, seven miles north-east of Ross-on-Wye, in the heart of the cider country and surrounded by old apple orchards for the production of scrumpy. The 13th-century church is thought to be a mere recent neighbour to the yew tree for some estimates put it at over 1,500 years old. Its hollow interior, complete with a wooden seat, has made it a very popular visitor attraction, so much so that there are concerns this could be to the detriment of the tree.

When exactly this seating was built isn't known, but a mention was made in *Littlebury's Directory and Gazetteer of Herefordshire* (1867–1877). Today it comprises three wooden seats, arranged in a U-shape, lining the inside of the trunk, where up to eight people can be accommodated. When approached from the rear, the enormous bulging, deeply fluted trunk, looking more like that of the tropical Banyan tree, is over eight metres in circumference and appears to be solid throughout. It is, therefore, hard to believe when the opposing side of the tree reveals a cavernous rotten interior.

Public access to ancient trees is very important to help nurture the appreciation and respect they fully deserve; however, getting the right balance between visitor numbers and the wellbeing and continued longevity of trees needs careful consideration. In recent years literature on yew trees has highlighted some of the more famous yews, such as the Much Marcle Yew, which has led to a greater number of visitors. Certainly, this present volume should also be considered guilty of this charge! In anticipation of damage being caused to the Much Marcle tree, especially through soil compaction caused by trampling feet, the yew was reported to the

Conservation Foundation as being in danger of suffering from 'visitor stress'. In response to this, various options were explored, including mulching around the base of the tree in order to feed its surface roots. Other options included erecting a protective fence around the trunk and the installation of a permanent wooden platform to mitigate soil compaction. One action that was taken in 2006 was a slight reduction of the crown weight, which resulted in the removal of about six tons of dead wood. As a result of this intervention, the tree looks markedly better, with much more new growth being produced.

As to its age, Peter Norton reporting on behalf of The Ancient Yew Group says: "An age of 1,500 seems to have become accepted for this tree. This originated in a certificate issued in the 1990s by the Conservation Foundation. It is, however, only an estimate, and the tree is probably much younger." Whatever its age, it will most likely be old enough to have witnessed the sound of an amazing nearby event known as 'The Wonder'. On the evening of 17th February 1775, three miles away, Marcle Hill was the centre of a massive landslide which took with it mature trees and buildings including the old Kinnaston Chapel. Today where this hill originally stood is a huge chasm over 120 metres in length and 12 metres deep, and the event is commemorated on a wall plaque at the appropriately named Slip Inn.

The Much Marcle Yew has survived all these events, and more to come. Sometime during the Victorian era, the branches of this female tree were supported by a metal frame to prevent them from falling to the ground where they would have eventually become rooted. Today, some of the Victorian lampposts that were used to support the drooping branches are still in place. One can only wonder if this intervention had not happened then perhaps we would today be admiring this tree as one of the famous walking yews.

The Muncaster Yew

I t is always a pleasure to have the opportunity to travel
through the magnificent landscapes that Cumbria has to offer;
certainly the dogged search for yew trees has taken me to
some remarkable locations within the Lake District National Park.
Of the 28 sites listed with Cumbrian ancient yews, there was only
room for trees from three locations in the Yew Conservation Hedge.
Included is the much-celebrated Martindale Yew that predates the
12th-century church that it overshadows; the famous Borrowdale
Yews that cling onto the sides of the tallest mountains in England
and, by contrast, the little-known tree in St Michael and All Angels'
churchyard surrounded by the splendour of the Muncaster Castle

estate. The magnificent castle sits at a pivotal point on the western Lake District coast, aloft a rocky outcrop above the River Esk, which sweeps round to join two other rivers that flow out into the Ravenglass estuary.

Muncaster Castle and Gardens is an established Royal Botanic Garden Edinburgh 'safe site' for conifers; trees started to be planted here by the International Conifer Conservation Programme in the 1990s. It was during a visit with Tom Christian in December 2008 to monitor these trees that we stumbled on the yew in the south-west corner of the churchyard of St Michael and All Angels. It was always a great education to be in the company of the ebullient Patrick Gordon-Duff-Pennington, the owner of Muncaster. Patrick was incredibly enthusiastic about the Gardens and greatly appreciated the unique collection of plants acquired from all over the world that grow so well in the extensive grounds, due to the benign influence of the Gulf Stream. He was keen to point out the yew tree, not especially for its stature as it is quite a modest specimen, but for the circular earthen mound (around eight metres in diameter and one metre high) that it sits upon. Patrick proudly gave an age of about 600 years for the tree, but what this was based on I am not sure. Up until then this yew tree was not on the list for inclusion in the Hedge, but Patrick's enthusiasm and historical knowledge of it convinced us that it had to be, and we immediately collected cuttings.

Subsequently I returned in 2021 to gather more research materials in conversation with Peter Frost-Pennington (Patrick's son-in-law). Peter pointed out that the form of the mound, and indeed its prominent location near the edge of an escarpment, is typical of the burial mounds known as barrows dating to the early Bronze Age (2000–1800 BCE). It is not unknown in England for churches to have been built on, or close to, prehistoric monuments, invariably accompanied by the planting of yew trees in order to sanctify them. The dedication to St Michael and All Angels is significant, since it is frequently associated with churches occupying sites with pagan connections. For example, the church of the same name in Northchapel, West Sussex, has a veteran yew tree planted on top of an earthen mound. There has been a church on the site at Muncaster since 1140, but the present small church dates from the 16th century. The landscape archaeologist who helped to compile an English Heritage report on Muncaster Castle (2011) spoke of the roadway past the church being very ancient, possibly prehistoric, and the earthen mound almost certainly as a pre-Christian ancient burial mound.

The female yew tree stands at 12 metres tall, but splits into several branches from about 1.5 metres from the ground and, similar to most old yew trees, the main trunk is developing a hollow. During a detailed analysis of the ancient yew trees of Cumbria in 1997, Graham Wilkinson gave a circumference of 4.3 metres when measured at 1.2 metres from the ground. Although of lesser significance, he listed three other yew trees nearby and also noted in his report of St Michael and All Angels, "Nice church with 'personality' in a pleasant setting by the castle". The health of all the yew trees in the churchyard is of concern, as they all show worrying signs of thinning crowns; some of the Irish yew trees are dying, one is dead. The Muncaster Yew would greatly benefit from having the invasive ivy, which has grown up into the canopy, removed. Such intervention will certainly give this ancient yew a better chance to face the challenges of the next few centuries.

The Selborne Yew

Founded in Saxon times, the Parish Church of St Mary's in the village of Selborne, Hampshire, is famous because of the yew tree that once stood in the churchyard, before it was blown down by a great gale in 1990. It came to fame through the writing of the celebrated 18th-century naturalist Rev. Gilbert White (1720–1793) who was curate of the church for many years.

Today, the tree survives as a lifeless stump covered in vegetation, but is survived by a clonal tree planted in the churchyard nearby.

The county of Hampshire is home to some of the UK's greatest yew trees; according to The Ancient Yew Group, it can boast 245 sites with trees of a considerable age, 67 of which occur in churchyards. Sadly, 16 of these trees have been lost, often as a result of felling due to a very risk-averse approach to health and safety.

Thanks to White's account of the Selborne yew tree, published in his seminal work *Natural History and Antiquities of Selborne* (1789), its celebrity status has long been assured, and that of yew trees in general. Such was the regard for this publication that it has never been out of print. Like so many clergymen of the day, White developed a profound knowledge of the natural world, and has been widely described as "a pioneer British Naturalist" and the "founding father of ecology". His literary skills have given us a taste of the once-mighty Selborne Yew:

"In the churchyard of this village is a yew tree whose aspect bespeaks it to be of great age: it seems to have seen several centuries, and is probably coeval with the church, and therefore may be deemed an antiquity: the body is squat, short and thick, and measures twenty-three feet in girth, supporting a head of suitable extent to its bulk. This is a male tree, which in the spring sheds clouds of dust and fills the atmosphere with its farina."

Several attempts have been made to age the Selborne Yew. From his observations of the nearby tree in the churchyard of All Saint's Church in Farringdon, White knew that the Selborne Yew was not the oldest in Hampshire. However, his growth measurements were used by the silviculturist Alan Mitchell, the first person to methodically measure trees in Britain and Ireland during the 1970s and 1980s, who gave an estimate of 1,400 years for the Selborne Yew. More recently, ring count studies of many hundreds of Hampshire stumps carried out by Toby Hindson have refined the estimate to between 1,150 and 1,200 years. This means that White was not far out when he said it was coeval with the church, which was built 941 years ago in 1180.

White would have been shocked and deeply saddened to have witnessed what happened at around 3.00pm on 25th January 1990, when the 'Burns Day Storm' ripped through the churchyard and uprooted the yew tree. For those who came to pay their respects, it was a devastating sight to see the focal tree of the churchyard strewn horizontally across the path, its gigantic trunk still encircled by the bench that was once the prime place to sit and contemplate this historic and peaceful space.

In the weeks following the great storm, attempts were made to reinstate the tree back to its original site. In excavating the planting hole, bones of about 30 skeletons were discovered; some were complete, dating back to about 1200 CE, and these were reinterred in the churchyard. On Tuesday 13th February 1990, watched by a large number of people, the tree was reinstated back in the original site using a winch and a crane. It was hoped that the tree would rejuvenate from the main trunk, but alas this was not to be, and in spring of 1992 the tree was officially announced as being dead. On 28th November 1992 a 60-centimetre tree was planted nearby in the churchyard, which was a clone collected from the original tree – this tree continues to flourish today. Using the same clonal material, trees have also been planted in other locations in England, including Bedgebury National Pinetum in Kent, which is the source of the plants in the Royal Botanic Garden Edinburgh's Yew Conservation Hedge.

Testament to its fame, in 2002 the Selborne Yew was declared one of the 50 trees chosen to mark the Queen's Golden Jubilee as

'Great British Trees'. This must be one of the few occasions when such an accolade has been bestowed on a dead tree. Today, the rotting trunk supports a fascinating array of wildlife, including wood-rotting fungi, epiphytic mosses and ferns – all food and drink to the keen naturalist! Surely, if Rev. Gilbert White were alive today, he would still be studying this tree and all its occupants.

The Stow-on-the-Wold Yews

No account of heritage yews should fail to mention these two remarkable trees, which dramatically flank the entrance to St Edward's Church in the market town of Stow-on-the-Wold, in the heart of the Cotswolds. The pair of yews could be at least 300 years old, but there is a paucity of information about them. Nevertheless, as with all yew trees, speculation abounds; as we shall see, many say that Tolkien sought inspiration from the doorway and the accompanying yews for his *The Lord of the Rings* trilogy.

The Gloucestershire church is not difficult to locate; once in the old square of Stow-on-the Wold, the distinctive 15th-century tower dominates the skyline, and access to the church is via a small alley called Church Lane. This Grade I-listed building is an ashlar Cotswold stone Norman church, parts of which date from the 11th or 12th century to the 14th century. It stands on the site of the original Saxon church that is believed to have been constructed from wood. Funds to build the tower and clerestory came from the community's wool trade. The church was renovated in the 17th century and again in 1873.

The pair of yew trees embrace the shallow north porch, which dates from the 17th century. Above the wooden, studded door are five small, colourful, stained-glass windows, and to complete this enchanting and mystical entrance is an oil lamp hanging in a prominent central position. There cannot be many other trees that have been planted so close to a church before. It is extraordinary that they continue to flourish in such proximity to a building; indeed, it is equally amazing that their root systems have not caused considerable damage to the foundations of the church. Both trees, which are male and therefore perhaps closely related, are similar in girth, one being 1.96 metres and the other 2.01 metres (measured at 1.22 metres from ground level). The fluted, polished trunks stretch out towards the base like huge, splayed paws and then suddenly disappear into the ground.

It is said that these two trees are all that is left of an avenue which once ran up to the doorway. An avenue of this nature is not unheard of – there is one of clipped yews that runs up to the front of St Mary's Church in Painswick. These avenues were not just planted as ornamental features; they served a purpose – it was from the church, through the avenue, that coffins were carried, and the yew tree represents hope and resurrection. The porch door was built about 300 years ago, and one assumes that the trees were planted either side soon after this.

The pair of yews that wrap themselves around the doorway command great attention from visitors to the churchyard – they must be some of the most frequently photographed yews in England. Many tourists have been drawn to these yew trees in the belief that J.R.R. Tolkien used the doorway to inspire the Doors of Durin in *The Lord of the Rings*. It is thought that while an academic at Oxford, Tolkien may have visited Stow-on-the-Wold during his time spent in the Cotswolds, where he frequently visited his brother in the nearby town of Moreton-in-Marsh. Tolkien took inspiration from many locations in the Cotswolds for his books, hence the speculation. Whatever the reality, the porch is known locally as 'The Yew Tree Door' or 'The Hobbit Door'. It is a very atmospheric doorway, especially on a misty winter's day, when the lamp above the porch is lit, reflecting on the polished trunks of the yews and the studded door. It entices the imagination to wonder what could await on the other side – perhaps a portal into a magical world!

The Taxal Yew

The Taxal church yew was chosen for inclusion in the Yew Conservation Hedge because it was thought that perhaps the name 'Taxal' was in some way connected to the previously mentioned anti-cancer drug Paclitaxel, which is sold under the brand name Taxol, approved for medical use in 1993. However, it is now understood that there is no link, as the place name of Taxal derives from 'tak' – a lease or tenure, and 'halh' – nook of land. This delightful Derbyshire village is located one mile south of the town of Whaley Bridge, within the Peak District National Park. The old yew tree stands at the top of an east-facing slope leading down to the River Goyt, in the small and very peaceful churchyard of St James' Church, which was formerly dedicated to St Leonard. Very little is known about this tree; but could it be coeval with the church, which dates back to the 12th century?

When I visited the female tree in February 2008, it was covered
with scarlet arils (fruits). In order to ensure the replication of the
same clone, vegetative material was collected mindful that seed-
set could have been the result of out-pollination with a nearby
male tree. The cuttings were placed in special bags, which are
impregnated with an anti-ageing compound, and these were
promptly taken to the village post office from where they were
dispatched for next day delivery to the propagation unit at the
Royal Botanic Garden Edinburgh.

There has been a church at Taxal since the 12th century, but like
so many old churches the present-day church has latterly been
enlarged and restored (mostly in the 17th and 19th centuries).
The Ancient Yew Group lists the Taxal yew as being 'Veteran',
which according to their classification means it is 500 years old or
more. The trunk is in the form of a hollow horseshoe shell from
which vigorous upright branches arise, and most recent records
give a girth of 4.7 metres in circumference.

Trunks of most very old yews, like many
ancient oaks, are hollow; hollowing is
a natural process caused by a wood-
decay fungus that digests moist wood,
causing it to rot. This is a very slow
process that can take centuries since
the wood is resinous and a limited
amount of water falls on the
trunk due to the protection
of the evergreen canopy.
Like all yews, the Taxal tree
is incredibly resistant to the
common dry rot honey fungus,
and the likelihood is that it has

become hollowed due to the action of the fungus known as 'chicken of the woods'.

The stone wall that encircles much of the trunk has been in place for a very long time, but the purpose of it is not entirely clear. Certainly it will not have been put in place to stop the much-loved donkeys from eating the poisonous foliage, although it is effective in doing so. Today three donkeys, Mary, Henry and Rodney (the latter being named after the local town councillor), form part of the maintenance team of volunteers that keep the grass of the churchyard in check during the summer months.

The Twyford Yew

The churchyard of St Mary's Church in the Hampshire village of Twyford is yet another location for an extraordinary and unusual yew tree. Thought to be about 450 years old, this distinctive tree stands to the north of the church, which dates back to Saxon times and is mentioned in the Domesday Book. One of four yews that grace this idyllic English churchyard, the tree has been skilfully clipped into the shape of a broad-based cone for more than 150 years, instead of being allowed to form a freely branching specimen.

There is little in-depth documentation concerning this yew tree; it only has brief treatment dating back to 1840 or possibly a little earlier. A cursory mention is given in *A topographical Dictionary of England* by Samuel Lewis (1858): "In the churchyard is an extraordinary yew-tree…" Then King & Murray (1865), in *A handbook for travellers in Surrey, Hampshire, and the Isle of Wight*, said of it: "In the churchyard there is a magnificent yew". Swanton (1958) makes the most significant contribution. In his modest but fascinating booklet entitled *The Yew Trees of England* he quotes information gleaned from Rev. J.R. Beynon in October 1954 who said: "It is on the north side of the present church… It is clipped annually, and there is no ceremony. There is a tradition of centuries of clipping. Just before the war it was examined by experts, who placed its age at 600 years at least, but its growth might have been stunted a bit by centuries of clipping, so it might be older." Rev. Beynon showed great interest in this unusual tree and in 1954 he measured its girth at 13 feet (3.6 metres). Because it is in a conservation area, the local council are required to apply for permission before cutting it.

In 1999 Tim Hills, from The Ancient Yew Group, made further measurements and mentions the bulging roots developing above the seat, which encircles the tree. This phenomenon has been noted with other yew trees when a seat is built closely around the girth, but it is more pronounced with the Twyford Yew. A bulging tree girth distorts the system for ageing trees, however if taken into account then this gives a measurement of 6.1 metres, although at the narrowest point the trunk is only 4.20 metres.

In September 2012, the *Twyford, Owslebury and Morestead Parish Magazine* ran a page-long article on the yew tree entitled 'A Secure Future for Twyford's Yew'. It was written by the Churchwarden Christopher Pope, who proudly reported on the Twyford tree being specially chosen for use in the Yew Conservation Hedge. He went on to say: "Drs Martin and Sabina Gardner called on us in April [2012] to take cuttings. It was a trip in which they had visited a churchyard in Sussex and Gilbert White's garden in Selborne. Martin took good-sized cuttings from our tree and secured them in his impressive travelling samples 'hold-all." It is heartening to see how much care and warmth there is for the yew tree by the church and its parishioners. In his article, Christopher Pope urged parishioners to visit the Royal Botanic Garden Edinburgh "to see the offspring from our yew growing in this other historic setting". On our visit to the tree in 2012 it was producing clouds of pollen, which confirmed the tree to be male.

Online, old images depicting this tree command relatively high prices. For example, at the cost of £61.99 one can purchase a black-and-white print depicting the yew tightly clipped and looking in its full splendour. Part of the caption says, "1,000 years old Yew Tree c.1955: The mighty yew tree in Twyford churchyard has a 15 ft [4.6 metres] circumference and is thought to be the oldest clipped yew in the country". In the church on the north aisle screen, there is a certificate signed by Robert Runcie (Archbishop of Canterbury 1980–1991) stating that the yew tree is over 450 years old. Certainly, this is a far more realistic age than estimates that creep up to 1,000 years or even more.

When the rebuilding of the church took place in 1878, 12 sarsen stones were discovered in the earlier Norman tower foundations. According to legend they were taken from a nearby hill before the first Saxon church was built. Therefore, although the yew was planted in Christian times, the site was most likely used for pre-Christian worship.

There is also a legend that speaks of a curious incident that happened on 7th October sometime during the 18th century.

It concerns the local man William Davies who, when riding across Twyford Down in dense fog, feared that he may fall into a chalk pit.

Thankfully he was saved by the sound of the church bells, which alerted him to change direction. As a mark of gratitude, he left in his will a sum of money to the pealers to ring the bells every 7th October, and I am assured that this tradition still continues today and is followed by a grand celebratory dinner.

The Llangernyw Yew

The Pulpit Yew

The Buttington Yew

Wales

Throughout Wales yew trees are a common sight, but as a native tree they are very infrequent. Perhaps the only location where they can be found in a natural woodland setting is on the Creuddyn Peninsula, in Marl Hall Woods, which has been designated a Site of Special Scientific Interest. The site overlooks the Conway estuary opposite the medieval town of Conway. Typically it occurs on limestone slopes where it is locally abundant, growing with ash and oak. Perhaps these yews are the mother trees of some of the 450 heritage yew trees cultivated in Wales. The Yew Conservation Hedge comprises trees collected from three Welsh heritage yews; like most of the yews in Wales, these all hail from churchyards.

The Llangernyw Yew

Deciding which of the yew trees from Wales to feature in the Yew Conservation Hedge proved a difficult choice, after all there were over 450 registered sites to consider! Incredibly, these sites include about 90 ancient yew trees, which means that they are 800 years or older. There is perhaps no other country in the world with a greater number of ancient trees – the vast majority grow in churchyards. Interestingly, unlike England, there are very few areas in Wales with naturally occurring native woodland due to a lack of suitable soil types.

The St Digain's Church yew in the remote Conwy village of Llangernyw lies between Llanrwst and Abergele above the Nant Rhan-hîr, a tributary of the River Elwy. Being one of the ten oldest yews in the British Isles and listed as one of 50 'Great British Trees' in celebration of the Queen's Golden Jubilee, it was an obvious yew to include in the Hedge. The popular headline age for this tree is from 4,000 to 5,000 years; indeed this is the age given on the churchyard gate in the form of a certificate issued by The Conservation Foundation as part of the Yew Tree Campaign, which ran from 1989 to 1999. However, a more realistic age is likely to be closer to 1,500 years, which is the same age as a nearby saint site; the church is dedicated to St Digain who was a 5th-century Welsh saint and Prince of Dumnonia (now known as the West Country).

Without doubt, the church is on an early medieval foundation, although the building standing today is thought not to be earlier than the 13th-century. The Grade II-listed church is quite small, well-proportioned and painted white. South of the church is a pair of standing stones, dating back anywhere between the 7th and 11th century, one of which has an incised cross.

Local folklore says that the ancient spirit known as Angelystor (the 'Recording Angel' or 'Evangelis' in Welsh) is present under the boughs of this old yew tree. It is said that on Halloween and 31st July the Angelystor appears in St Digain's Church and solemnly announces in Welsh the names of parishioners who will die shortly after.

According to folklore, on one Halloween a tailor called Shôn ap Robert refuted the idea of Angelystor while drinking in a local pub. His fellow drinkers suggested he visit the church to see if the story was groundless, but on his arrival at the church door, he heard a loud voice mention his name to which he retorted "Hold, hold, I am not ready yet!" but alas, he died later that year.

Poet Margaret Sandbach (1812–1852), who lived in nearby Hafodunos Hall and is buried at St Digain's Church, described a funeral here in 1852:

"I was walking down to the village one day in the spring – there had been a heavy shower, and a beautiful and striking scene met my eye as I approached the church. There was a funeral – and under the old yew tree a dark group of mourners had gathered around the grave – a gleam of light fell upon the spot – a rainbow made a bright arch above, and the misty shower was fading away on the hills. Earth and heaven seemed blended then – the dark group below – the brightness above. It was perfectly calm too, and not a sound disturbed the solemnity of the scene..."

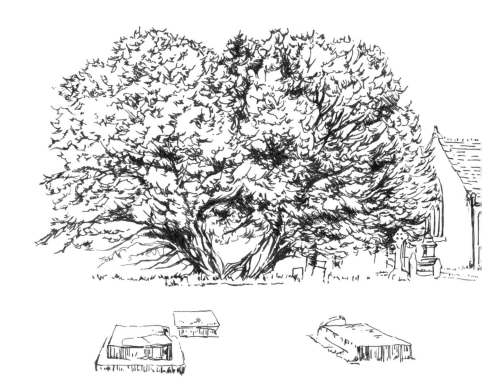

The magnificent tree that graces this churchyard has a very distinctive shape. Its huge, deep green, spreading crown falls low to the ground. A fragmented trunk comprising four low, wide-spreading stems, with the centre long since gone, supports this monumental tree. In recent years, one fragment has become lowered and is now resting on the ground, but without any noticeable root movement. Such structural repositioning is an integral part of a yew's journey through life and adds to the idiosyncratic character of the tree. These remarkable trees need to be left well alone to allow them to take on their own natural form and evolve – we must sometimes put our horticultural and arboricultural practices to one side. In the 18th century markets were held around the tree, with stalls in the cemetery, meat hanging in the church porch and people smoking and drinking at the altar – thankfully times have changed! Its recent publicity has earned this tree the respect that it clearly deserves; a rusting oil tank that was incongruously being stored in the hollow of the tree has now been removed.

The Buttington Yew

T he small Welsh village of Buttington, known by the Welsh name Tal y Bont (meaning, 'the end of the bridge'), lies two miles from Welshpool, in Powys. During the Saxon era it was called Butdigingtune and was the site of a desperate battle fought between an alliance of Anglo-Saxons and Welsh against the invading Danish army in 894. The battle, in which the Danes were eventually defeated and driven out, was in sight of All Saints Church where the magnificent ancient Buttington yew tree still flourishes today.

In 1838, when the construction of Buttington Trewern County Primary School encroached into the south-east corner of the churchyard, a grim discovery of a large quantity of skulls was made, thought to be those of the soldiers who fought in the bloody battle of Buttington. To mark the site of the battle a pedunculate oak (*Quercus robur*) was said to have been planted by local people. The Buttington Oak, as it became known, was planted close to Offa's Dyke, an ancient Roman pathway marking the border between Wales and England. When it was finally ravaged by unrelenting storms in 2017, it had a girth of 11 metres, making the tree the second-largest oak in Wales. Interestingly, when mycologists analysed the fungus flora of the rotten core wood, they discovered a fungus hitherto unknown and named it *Ypsilina buttingtonensis*.

One could speculate that if a yew tree had been planted to commemorate the battle, then it may well still exist today, as yews are far more resilient. Yes, even more resilient than the mighty oak! Yew trees are the ultimate specialists in survival because of their ability to regenerate, which is why they are often referred to as being eternal. At almost any stage in its life, a yew tree is capable of vigorous regeneration, and it can cope with even the most severe mechanical damage caused by storms.

The tree in the churchyard of All Saints Church is in its 'hollow tree stage' of life; for nearly all other native tree species in the British Isles this would be a near end-of-life phase, but not for this yew or any other yew at the same stage of their life cycle. It has a thin skin of living tissue, the all-important cambium layer, with a single break in the trunk of about 90 centimetres across. In 2008, the tree had a girth measurement of 8.15 metres at ground level. Although completely hollowed out, the trunk and supporting structures maintain a full and healthy crown.

The girth growth rate remains high – for example, it has increased by ten centimetres in less than ten years – and this is important because it re-distributes weight pressures. Eventually this tree will lose its crown, the trunk will become a shell and the final stage will be a ring of vertical fragments, which may take the appearance of independent trees but still share the same root system.

The small, single-chambered church of All Saints is such an impressive structure, although some of its charm has perhaps been lost by being hemmed in on two sides by major roads, one of which is the main Shrewsbury to Welshpool road (A458). The whitewashed building, with its slate roof, is thought to date back to the 14th or 15th century, and certainly there has been a church on the present site from at least 1265, when it was part of the Manor of Strata Marcella.

The statuesque yew tree lies to the west of the church close to the churchyard's southern boundary, now marked by re-sited memorial slabs. The tree stands so proudly and dominates the very small, slightly raised churchyard. At first sight, one is forgiven for thinking the tree has been planted inside a circular, neatly clipped yew hedge, but on closer inspection, one can see the mass of foliage grows directly from the main trunk. These shoots have arisen from epicormic buds which lie just beneath the bark, triggered into active growth to form shoots when, for instance, damage occurs to the upper part of the tree. Epicormic shoots are how trees regrow after coppicing or pollarding, or even fire. The classic British native tree, which produces copious amounts of epicormic growth, is the linden or lime tree (*Tilia*). These epicormic growths are a welcome sight as they root more readily and can produce erect leading shoots, which encourages the development of upright growth. So, it was from these shoots that propagation material was selected and placed in stay-fresh salad bags. These special bags are impregnated with a preservative, which helps to keep the cuttings in prime condition until they can be processed in the Royal Botanic Garden Edinburgh Nursery.

The Pulpit Yew

Most commuters hurtling along the North Wales Expressway (A55) are perhaps oblivious to the beautiful landscapes and the charm afforded by the many hamlets and villages in the Vale of Clwyd. Less than 12 miles from this busy highway, which runs from Chester to Holyhead, is the Parish Church of Nantglyn where one can discover the extraordinary Pulpit Yew. The Clwyd village of Nantglyn lies four miles south-east of the medieval town of Denbigh; it is easily missed amongst the entanglement of narrow country lanes that dissect the rural landscape, overlooked by the lofty peaks of the Snowdonia National Park. Typically, for November (2011), the weather was very damp and cold when I visited this small Welsh village. The church of St James, where the Pulpit Yew grows, is by the small stream of Afon Ystrad, which flows eastwards from the foothills of Mynydd Hiraethog; Nantglyn literally means 'stream in the valley'.

Of all the sites on the heritage yews target list for the Yew Conservation Hedge, it was the Pulpit Yew that I perhaps most looked forward to seeing. Although this was my first visit to the remote village of Nantglyn, I was familiar with one of its famous past residents, David Samwell (1751–1798), who was the son of the local vicar, William Samwell. As an avid reader of natural history travel, I was aware of David Samwell, a surgeon on board *HMS Resolution*, the Royal Navy sloop in which the explorer Captain James Cook made voyages of exploration around the world between 1776 and 1779. During his time spent on board as surgeon, Samwell also wrote poetry and kept a detailed journal of his travels, including recording the death of Captain Cook in Kealakekua Bay in Hawaii at the hands of disgruntled local people.

The Muckcross Abbey Yews

The Crom Yews

The Irish Yew

The Yellow-Fruited Yew

Ireland

There is a strong association between Ireland and the yew, indeed there is substantial evidence that Ireland derives its name from *iwo-eru* or *iw-er* meaning 'yew land' in old Irish. Furthermore, at least 17 Irish townlands have names that mean 'church of the yew'. It is even suggested that rather than the sessile oak being considered as the national tree of the Republic of Ireland, it should in fact be the yew. Today, native Irish populations of yew are restricted to south-western Ireland where limestone outcrops occur – this is a classic habitat for the species. Included in the Yew Conservation Hedge are trees collected from a single woodland on the Muckross Peninsula within the Killarney National Park. Yew was an important and sacred tree in early Ireland, with a particular association with church sites. However, only around 100 heritage yews are recorded for Ireland and of these, three were chosen for the Hedge.

NATIVE YEWS
The Reenadinna Yews

Yew woodland in Ireland is very restricted in its distribution and today threatened by severe browsing pressures from rabbits and deer. As mentioned above, it is only found in about seven locations on limestone outcrops in the south-western part of the country. The most extensive remaining area is Reenadinna woodland, which is a 25-hectare site on the eastern end of the Muckross Peninsula in the heart of the Killarney National Park. This is the park's rarest habitat, set in a very picturesque landscape. It was from this woodland that Tom Christian and I sampled seed in 2009.

This was my second visit to this remarkable forest. It is known for its incredibly dense canopy, which mostly excludes other tree species, except for holly and, in areas where conditions are lighter, hazel. The most striking aspect of the forest is the limestone reefs on which the woodland grows – the forest floor is strewn with large boulders covered in mats of bright green mosses. In some instances, the yew trees are growing out of very tight rock fissures. The trees vary from six to fourteen metres in height and recent research has established that the oldest are about 250 years old.

Yew is considered to be the most browse-sensitive species in the Killarney woodlands. Some trees have been killed by deer constantly rubbing their antlers on the base of the trees. As a result of the harmful effects of grazing animals, areas within the woodland were enclosed by a fence in 1969.

However, regeneration still remains poor due to the dense shade cast by the yew canopy. When we visited the forest, seed production was very poor and we only managed to find four trees to make collections from. Seed germination also proved to be poor – 12 trees have been planted in the Yew Conservation Hedge.

HERITAGE YEWS

The Irish Yew

This strange, upright form of the European yew was originally found in the mountains of County Fermanagh in Northern Ireland. It is better known than any other yew tree in the world; certainly, nearly every public garden and churchyard in Britain and Ireland will have at least one specimen. Today the mother tree stands in the grounds of Florence Court, not far from where it was originally discovered in 1767.

The European yew (*Taxus baccata*) has given rise to over 100 horticultural named novelties (cultivars), which are often seen in formal gardens, especially in dwarf conifer collections. These plants, which look different from the mother plant, arise due to a genetic mutation, which is exactly what has happened with the Irish yew. The discovery of this very distinctive yew is well documented and begins 255 years ago in 1767. A local farmer, George Willis, was hare coursing among shrubs of juniper at Carraig-na-madadh' ('the rock of the dog') en route to the summit of Cuilcagh. To his amazement,

Willis stumbled upon two yew seedlings that looked very different to the typical yew, with an erect and rigid habit. Without hesitation he transplanted them – one went to his own cottage garden, and one was given to his landlord, Viscount Mount Florence, for planting in the demesne at Florence Court.

It was some decades before the full extent of the habit of this new variant was observed in the tree growing at Florence Court. But the flourishing tree soon caught the attention of the visiting public and indeed of the horticultural community, who are always keen to find novel growth forms. Cuttings were taken and distributed to other gardens and soon it gained wider recognition. It also started to gain the attention of botanists, and some considered it so different that they suggested it should be treated as a new species under the Latin name of *Taxus hibernica*. Eventually, it was decided it was an unusual form of the common yew and has since become known as *Taxus baccata* 'Fastigiata'. The first printed description of the Irish yew, which has spirally arranged deep green leaves and erect shoots, was in 1812, published in Edward Wakefield's *Account of Ireland*. It read – "I observed at this place [Florence Court] a yew tree growing in a spiral form like a cypress: it is a native of the rock on the adjacent mountains".

This Irish yew was even grown by Charles Darwin and in a letter to his very close botanical friend, Joseph Dalton Hooker in 1845, the father of evolution makes mention of the Irish yew: "I know nothing, (I wish I did) on sexes of Irish Yew, but I observe all my young trees bear berries; I had thoughts of going to the Nursery & looking to the trees. I will try to get enquiries made at Florence Court."

It was not until 1818, when the tree became widely available in commercial horticultural circles, that it was first listed in the catalogue of Conrad Loddiges. This very notable 18th- and 19th-century plant nursery, based in Hackney, London, traded in exotic plants throughout Europe. By the middle of the 19th century, it was through such outlets that the Irish yew became widely available and started to be planted in graveyards, cemeteries, parklands and landscaped gardens. In 1863, it received the Royal Horticultural Society's prestigious 'First Class Certificate'. The Irish yew is female and has very attractive coral-red cones; however, other forms have arisen, including a male plant with yellow margins to its leaves, known as the Golden Irish yew (*Taxus baccata* 'Fastigiata Aureomarginata'). Because of its disciplined shape it has become a favourite when designing avenues, for creating very effective vistas. Two examples can be seen in County Down: one at Hillsborough Castle and the other leading to the Parliament building at Stormont outside of Belfast.

The plants in the Yew Conservation Hedge show the typically densely upright columnar habit, especially when young. If allowed to form a tree, they become more broadly conical; the original tree at Florence Court has formed a widely spreading habit, but still with very bolt-upright shoots, especially when they are young – it has to be said that, in my opinion, this is not the most attractive of trees.

The Crom Yews

The ruins of the Old Crom Castle are located along the shores of Upper Lough Erne in the south of County Fermanagh in Northern Ireland. It is a unique and tranquil setting, with two low-spreading old yew trees standing very close to each other near to the crumbling walls of the castle. The trees, one male and one female, are clearly of different ages and estimates put them anywhere from 300 to 800 years old, but perhaps a more realistic age is at the lower end of this range. Whatever their ages they are celebrated as being some of the oldest trees in Northern Ireland.

The Crom Estate is just one of 20 sites where heritage yews can be found in Northern Ireland. It was gifted to the National Trust by the 6th Earl of Earne in 1987, and is one of three sites in County Fermanagh where old yew trees still stand today. This 800-hectare demesne, which is now a nature reserve protecting one of the few Irish stands of native broadleaved woodlands, has been an important sanctuary for two of Ireland's famous and much-cherished yew trees. Unlike the Republic of Ireland, where yews are native, here in Northern Ireland there are no stands of yew which are thought to be indigenous.

The Old Castle at Crom was built at the beginning of the 17th century by Michael Balfour, a Scottish planter from Fife. The castle survived two sieges by the Jacobites in 1689 and was accidentally gutted by fire in 1764. One assumes that the yew trees, which are said to predate the building, escaped these disturbing events unscathed. In 1840 the present-day Crom Castle was built. This majestic building stands about a kilometre north of the Old Crom Castle and the accompanying pair of yew trees.

When viewed from afar, these two inseparable trees form a low, wide-spreading canopy. Clearly the male tree to the left is much taller and in 2000 it was measured at a height of 14 metres, while the smaller female tree was 10.8 metres. Today, under the canopy there is sufficient light to see the remarkable twisted and contorted branches, which have become intertwined and radiate in all directions. Many have become grafted together, forming a conglomerate of indefinable shapes. Some of the more robust branches have taken the form of a boa constrictor, weaving and twining around other branches and eventually snaking out onto the ground where some have become rooted. The larger male tree has numerous, very robust branches that grow bolt upright out of the crown. The bark is reddish-brown with purple tones, and in places is flaking or even peeling. The trees are planted on small mounds, which is thought to be evidence that this is a pre-Christian site and was considered sacred, forming a centre for pagan ceremonies.

At one time, the horizontal branches were lifted from the ground and supported on 32 brick pillars, but these were replaced by oak posts in 1833. The canopy was trained for topiary. Under the canopy, with a spread of almost 23 metres across, were laid gravel

paths which provided the ideal location for dining parties, with, some say, gatherings of up to 200 people. One can only imagine what a unique and special venue this must have been, and what one might hear if only today the watchful yew trees could reveal some of the intriguing and perhaps scandalous conversations being had beneath the yews' entangled branches.

The Muckcross Abbey Yews

The demesne of the Franciscan abbey at Muckross in Killarney National Park, County Kerry, has two fine male yew trees very worthy of inclusion in the Yew Conservation Hedge. The most famous yew rises majestically from the centre of the cloisters of the ruined abbey, while the other stands close by, just outside of the walls. Both are thought to have been planted when the abbey was constructed and therefore date back to the 15th century.

It is the tree confined in the tight space of the cloisters of the abbey that receives the most attention. Opinion is divided concerning the age of this tree; nevertheless, it is believed to be one of the oldest yews on the island of Ireland. John Lowe, the great authority of the day, in *The Yew Trees of Great Britain and Ireland* (1897), doubted its great age saying, "there could not well be found a more striking instance of the error of assuming a tree is of the same age as the building near which it grows. It was probably, in 1780, less than two hundred years old." This was in response to John Loudon (1783–1843), who writes of the yew in his celebrated work *Arboretum et Fructicetum Britannicum* as being "upwards of seven hundred years old". More recently, Charles Nelson in *Trees of Ireland* (1993), typically didn't pull any punches when he wrote "Claims that it is over one thousand years old are ridiculous". He goes on to say: "Inspection shows that it is standing exactly in the centre of the courtyard, and the logical conclusion is that the tree was planted therein, as an ornament, after the completion of the building in the fifteenth century". This would make the tree around 500 years old.

In 1883, an effusive account about the tree was published in the *Dublin Penny Journal*: "It is preserved with religious veneration by the peasantry; and so awful is the effect produced on the mind by its extraordinary canopy, that many persons shrink back with terror on entering within its precincts, and few can remain long without feeling an impatient desire to escape from its oppressive influence". This is indeed a unique tree, not just for its location, but for the extraordinary reddish gnarled trunk that twists and spirals in a way similar to that of a sweet chestnut. Standing on a small mound, the trunk, which is 3.3 metres in circumference, is clear of any branches for about 4.2 metres in height, at which point it branches out up through the ruinous walls of the abbey.

It will perhaps be of no surprise that such a location is steeped in legends, and to this end, in his authoritative work *Heritage Trees of Ireland* (2013), Aubrey Fennell revealed that the tree was planted on the grave of a monk who had been absent for 100 years, and finally returned there to die. Fennell also tells of a legend that an image of the Virgin Mary is buried underneath the tree and that anyone who attempts to damage the yew will die within a year. Apparently, this warning was ignored by a soldier "who hacked off a small branch which dripped blood. He promptly dropped dead on the spot".

We should not forget the nearby yew, which lies just outside the confines of the abbey, growing within a stone wall. With a trunk of four metres circumference, this tree has a far greater stature than that of the more celebrated tree within the abbey cloisters.

The Yellow-Fruited Yew

The island of Ireland is not especially well known for its very old yew trees; certainly none compares with the ancient trees found in England, Scotland and Wales. In fact, according to The Ancient Yew Group, of around 100 heritage yew trees in Ireland, none are classified as being 'Ancient' (trees 800 years or more old and with a girth in excess of seven metres). Yew trees associated with religious sites are also relatively infrequent. Again, taking data from The Ancient Yew Group, just 11 religious sites are recorded.

Only one other tree from the Republic of Ireland has been included in The Yew Conservation Hedge. This is the named cultivar *Taxus baccata* 'Fructu Luteo' which has very striking yellow 'fruits'. This was first observed in about 1817 on the demesne of the Bishop of Kildare at Glasnevin near Dublin; but according to Mackay in his *Flora Hibernica* (1836) cultivated stock had come from a tree at Clontarf Castle in Dublin. The tree is of modest proportions, standing three metres tall and spreading (largely on one side only) to about 4.5 metres. Material for the Hedge was collected from an old tree in the National Botanic Gardens, Glasnevin, in Dublin. Dr Matthew Jebb, Director of the garden, suggests the tree was planted sometime between 1880 and the 1920s.

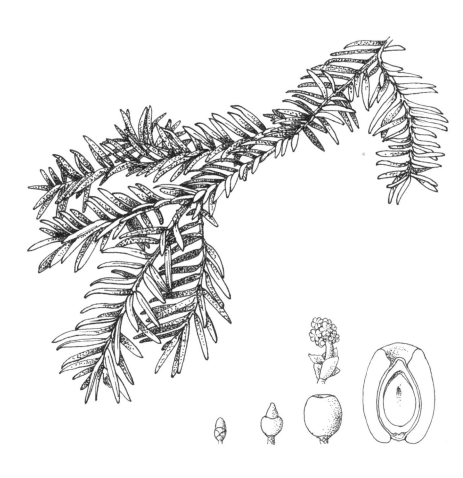

The other
countries represented
in the Hedge

ALBANIA

The European yew is infrequent in Albania, which was confirmed
when I visited the country at the beginning of September 2009.
Not only was this my first visit to this little-known part of the world,
but it was the first time in the 350-year history of the Royal Botanic
Garden Edinburgh for any member of staff to undertake botanical
fieldwork in Albania. For this significant event I was joined by two
members of staff from the Garden: Horticultural Instructor
Laura Cohen, and Agron Shehi from the Estates Services Team.
Agron, an Albanian national, proved to be vital not only for his
language skills but also as an exceptional tree climber. Our hosts
were Dr Marash Rakaj from the University of Shkodra, and
Dr Petrit Hoda, Curator of The Botanical Gardens of Tirana.

With more than 70 per cent of its territory covered by mountains,
Albania is one of the most mountainous countries in Europe.
We had a taste of this when we visited the remarkable Albanian Alps

in the north of the country, which form the southernmost part of the Dinaric Alps. This is one of Europe's most rugged mountain ranges, which encompasses Kosovo, Montenegro and Albania. Here, yew trees can form pure small stands; but alas, our search was in vain, for after several days of looking not a single tree was located.

As a result of this, our attention was then concentrated in the south-west of the country, along the Albanian Riviera in the Ceraunian Mountains within the Llagora National Park. Here, at an elevation of almost 1,000 metres, we found several hundred yew trees growing with other conifers such as the black pine and the King Boris fir. We collected seed from outlying yew trees, which were thought to be at greatest risk of loss; these were between 2.5 and 8 metres tall. The ten trees we collected seed from had cut branches; some were in quite a mutilated state, and one tree had recently been cut to the ground. Yew wood is still revered in Albania for its fine qualities in furniture making. Thankfully, the Yew Conservation Hedge is acting as a safe haven for 73 trees as a result our seed collections.

CROATIA

Croatia is notable for its forested landscape, with 46 per cent of the country covered by forest. The most common species are beech and oak, which are sometimes intermixed with conifers such as the European fir. The European yew is not commonly encountered, and when they are they form small patches mixed in with beech and sometimes limes. As in so much of its natural range, the yew is in a steep decline in Croatia due to the high value of its timber for use in the furniture-making industry. It was highly appropriate that the botanical fieldwork in Croatia was undertaken by Vlasta Jamnický, the Interpretation Manager at the Royal Botanic Garden Edinburgh, and her father Vlado Jamnický, both Croatian nationals. They were assisted in Croatia by Dr Zelimir Borzano from the Faculty of Forestry, University of Zagreb.

For the Yew Conservation Hedge we chose one of Croatia's most-threatened populations in the Papuk Geopark, which lies in the Slavonia Region in the north-east corner of Croatia. This area is known for its very picturesque landscape, with the 954-metre limestone peak of Papuk towering above large tracts of deciduous and evergreen forest. At one time yews were relatively common in this area, with four noted locations. However, today there is just one location left, which has only 20 trees in two closely separated groves. This location for yews, which covers 0.72 of a hectare, was protected in 2005 as a Natural Monument. The habitat is on a north-facing slope, which is dominated by European fir, beech, and in places common hazel. The forest is typically dense and grows in shallow soil over a substrate of limestone. The trees vary from eight to fifteen metres tall; most occur as multi-stemmed trees or even large shrubs. In all, seed was collected from seven trees and seed from six of these germinated, which has resulted in 37 trees being planted in the Hedge.

CZECH REPUBLIC

Yew has a relatively widespread distribution in the Czech Republic; in fact, a survey conducted from 2000 to 2001 found that there are just over 11,000 trees. In some locations there is a noticeable lack of old-growth trees because of selective logging for their highly prized timber. The trees have a broad altitudinal range from sea level, where it is associated with oak, to 900 metres where it grows with spruce and beech. However, most trees are found at 500 metres where they happily share a habitat with oak and beech trees.

The trees in the Yew Conservation Hedge were collected as seed from Domažlice District, which is on the western border of the Czech Republic and almost 150 kilometres west of Prague. I travelled to the small town of Kanice in December 2009 with Royal Botanic Garden Edinburgh botanist Sabina Knees, where we met up with Zdeněk Blahník, a honeysuckle specialist from the Department of Forestry, in the Ministry of Agriculture of the Czech Republic. We spent a very cold day on the nearby Mt Netřeb. There had been heavy overnight snow, which made conditions even more challenging.

The 200 trees on the northern slopes of the small mountain are protected in Reserve Netřeb; they have ages varying from 300 to 700 years old and are thus some of the oldest yew trees in the country. The slopes where they grow have a mixture of lime, oak, and sycamore. Some commercial exotic species such as Scots pine are also present. Here we collected seed from six trees, with some of them measuring heights of 15 metres. We also visited a small forest 66 kilometres north-east of Mt Netřeb in the Prírodní Reserve V Horách. The reserve has a population of about 100 trees growing with silver fir, but due to the lack of seed only one tree (15 metres tall) was sampled. Our collections have resulted in 86 trees being planted in the Hedge.

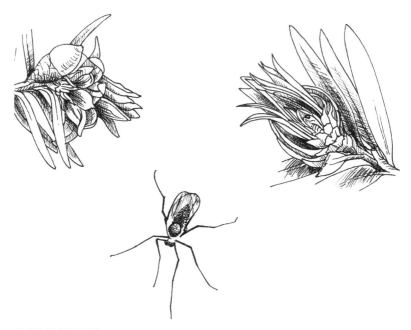

DENMARK

Compared with the other Nordic countries of Norway, Finland and Sweden, the occurrence of yew in Denmark has always been sporadic. The two remnant forests of Munkebjerg Strandskov and Marselisborg Skov, which stand about 65 kilometres apart in Jutland, are all that have survived. The latter is bordered by the city of Aarhus and is intensively managed. It consists of scattered trees, none of which exceed 2.5 metres in height; however, self-sown yew seeds from neighbouring gardens are polluting the natural gene pool. The forest at Munkebjerg Strandskov, near to Vejle, is more natural and because of this it was decided to collect seed from this location for the Yew Conservation Hedge. This was another opportunity to choose a member of Royal Botanic Garden Edinburgh staff who is a national of a country where collections were required, and to this end the tropical botanist Dr Axel Poulsen undertook the botanical fieldwork in October 2010.

The forest of Munkebjerg Strandskov covers an area of 800 hectares and occurs in hilly terrain with steep slopes. It is a mosaic of managed beech forest and conifer plantation; the native yew population occurs in gullies in the north-eastern corner of the forest. The yew population was first discovered in 1865 and has been protected by law since 1933. When it was first discovered it consisted of low trees, which had been heavily pruned. Thankfully, today the population is in a much healthier state with trees up to 19 metres tall. Further encouragement is that the population has increased, from less than 200 trees in 1925, to more than 2,000 in 1998. This increase is thought to be due to a thinning of the forest canopy, which has encouraged seedling establishment. Crucially, there is no evidence of rabbit or deer browsing, which is one of the biggest threats to native yew populations. Seed was collected from ten trees, which have given rise to 70 trees being planted in the Hedge.

GEORGIA

The European yew has an extensive distribution in Georgia, with most populations concentrated in the east of the country, and it is from here that the collections for the Hedge were made. In 2010, Richard Brown, Senior Horticulturist at the Royal Botanic Garden Edinburgh, spent a week in dramatic limestone mountainous surroundings accompanied by Dr Manana Khutsishvili who is Head of the National Herbarium of Georgia at Tbilisi Botanical Garden.

Richard, who has also made collections of yews from Russia and Ukraine, organised the botanical fieldwork in Georgia as he had a good working knowledge of the country having visited on several occasions to study its rich alpine flora. He remembers from these previous visits seeing scattered yew trees on steep mountain slopes, which represented a fraction of their former population sizes. However, now with the assistance of Dr Khutsishvili, he was taken to some remarkable locations where yew occurs in pristine protected areas. These included the National Parks of Borjomi-Kharagauli, Kolkheti and Tbilisi, the last of which has extensive beech forests with yew growing close to the Martqopi monastery. This 6th-century building is dramatically positioned on limestone outcrops, which rise out of dense forested slopes of the Lalno Mountain range at an altitude of 1,350 metres.

Collections were also made in the Batsara Reserve where it is thought that the largest stands of yew trees in the world occur. This important protected area was first established as a reserve in 1935, specifically to safeguard the yews. Today, the trees are distributed over an area of 800 hectares mainly in association with field maple, hornbeam, and common ash, but dominated by Oriental beech. Here yews can be found in pure stands covering a 200-hectare area. The average age of the trees is thought to be almost 1,000 years old; however, some of the old-growth trees have been estimated to be between 1,500 and 1,800 years old.

The yew collections from Georgia came from five different locations with seed being collected from 25 trees, which has resulted in 160 trees being planted in the Hedge.

HUNGARY

There are several records of yews growing in Hungary, but some of these are thought not to be truly native and have been planted, or become naturalised, from cultivated sources. The non-poisonous, red fleshy aril of the fruits of yew are very attractive to hungry birds or even to badgers during the cold winter months, and can be very readily dispersed from non-native trees.

There are just two locations in Hungary where native yew trees grow, and these are confined to the Bükk Mountains, which form part of the Inner Carpathian Mountains in the north of the country, and the Bakony Mountains in western Hungary. In October 2009, dendrologist Dr István Rácz, who is curator of the Hungarian Natural History Museum, Budapest, undertook the seed collections of yew from the Bakony Mountains aided by colleagues and National Park officials.

The Bakony Mountain range covers over 4,000 square kilometres and since 2015 has been designated a UNESCO Global Geopark. The yew population of about 13,000 trees is thought to be one of the largest in central Europe and covers an area of around 287 hectares. The collections were concentrated on Mt Miklóspál, which is covered by beech-dominated forest. Even though the area has protection, the all-important process of regeneration is thwarted by deer browsing the seedlings. In his field notes István observed that bark and branches had been damaged by deer browsing and went on to say "it was as if the deer were addicted to eating the yews".

The Bakony Mountains are one of Europe's celebrated centres for hunting, and deer form an important part of this tradition. However, there has to be a delicate balance between these traditional activities and forest conservation. István reported that seed was scarce, but in the end ten trees were sampled which has yielded 24 trees for planting in the Yew Conservation Hedge.

MOROCCO

It may be of some surprise that the southernmost distribution of the European yew extends as far south as North Africa, but indeed it can be found in some remote mountainous forested habitats of Morocco (and Algeria). Recent research has established that it has a discontinuous distribution, following the main 2,500-kilometre-long mountain range of the mighty Atlas Mountains that separates the Mediterranean and the Atlantic coastlines from the Sahara Desert.

There is also a distribution of trees along the Rif Mountains of northern Morocco which form the greater part of its 290-kilometre length; the range hugs the Mediterranean Sea. In Morocco, yew is found in 34 different locations, of which recent research has managed to locate 27. On my visit to Morocco I was accompanied by Tom Christian; our in-country expert was Dr Mostafa Lamrani-Alaoui from the National Forestry School of Engineers at Rabat University.

In the High Atlas, yew occurs sparsely in small stands of trees, most of which have been subject to cutting for firewood. In the Middle Atlas it is more frequent and grows in larger stands. For example, we found it in a stand of about 50 trees on a very steep bank leading down to a mountain river. It was growing with isolated

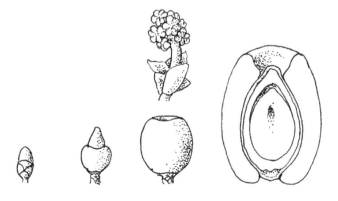

trees of the Atlas cedar. In one location, it was growing in a deep sinkhole, clinging to the steep craggy slopes. Sadly, our collections from the Middle Atlas had to be discarded as we realised that the permission to collect was in the end not forthcoming. Our attention then turned to the Rif Mountains where there are 13 localities with yew trees. This is the wettest part of Morocco, with a rainfall of over one metre per annum. Yew occurs as single trees, or in small groups, growing with the Moroccan fir and the Atlas cedar. Our collections came from the eastern end of the Rif mountains, where we collected from nine trees; from this 290 trees have been planted, the greatest number from any country represented in the Yew Conservation Hedge.

NORWAY

It is not only the European yew that has its absolute northerly distribution in Norway, but a host of other familiar trees and shrubs such as holly, hazel, small-leaved lime, beech and Wych elm. The occurrence of such species here is thought to be as a result of the warm Atlantic Ocean current that originates in the Gulf of Mexico, known as the Gulf Stream, that skirts the west coast of Norway. In Norway, yew is predominantly restricted to coastal areas of western and southern parts of the country. Even though it is relatively abundant throughout its range, it is still Red Listed in Norway as Vulnerable, mainly due to the lack of regeneration as a consequence of deer browsing.

In order to obtain seed from the most northerly location for the European yew, Tom Christian travelled to the remote island of Otrøya, off the coast of Central Norway. The population contains just over 20 individuals scattered along a narrow strip of woodland close to the coastline, where it grows with Scots pine, silver birch, hazel, holly and rowan. The yew trees, which are often growing from the base of rocks near to the shoreline, vary from deer-browsed, multi-stemmed trees two to three metres tall, to more robust trees up to five metres tall. Seed was collected from a total of 13 trees and of these 68 are now planted in the Yew Conservation Hedge.

Interestingly, Tom visited both the northernmost population here in Norway and the southernmost, in the Middle Atlas Mountains in Morocco, and was therefore able to compare these two extremes. In Norway, the yews grow on a south-facing slope more or less at sea level; in Morocco, they grow in valleys and in craters in the Middle Atlas Mountains, where they are sheltered from the sun, nearly 2,000 metres above sea level. In approximately the same locations both in Norway and Morocco, other familiar tree species such as hazel, holly and hawthorn have either their northern or southern limit, or both.

POLAND

The distribution of yews in Poland has been intensively studied; we now have a very clear overview of the populations, even down to their genetic structure. In all, there are 31 populations collectively comprising over 25,500 individual trees. Nine populations have over 1,000 trees, with one having as many as 5,500. Most have less than 500 trees and seven have 100 or less.

Even with these relatively large numbers, regeneration within these forests is under threat due to browsing; this is still the case even though nearly all populations are under some sort of protection. Tom Christian was joined by Dr Grzegorz Iszkuło of the Institute of Dendrology, Polish Academy of Sciences, University of Zielona Góra, in order to make collections from two Polish populations.

The first of these was the well-known Wierzchlas Reserve, located in northern Poland about 40 kilometres to the west of the Vistula River, in the southern Pomeranian Lake District. This magnificent

reserve, comprising a rich woody flora, was established in 1956. With over 3,500 individuals, it is Poland's largest stand of yew trees and is mixed with sycamore, limes and sometimes with very old Scots pine trees. The population has a healthy level of regeneration, but seedlings perish in parts of the forest where light levels are low.

There is a similar situation with the second population visited, at Cisowa Góra in the Sudety mountains of southern Poland. The population here, which extends to almost 19 hectares with over 750 mature individuals, is constantly at risk from deer. Many of the tree trunks are protected by plastic netting, and seedlings are surrounded by cages in an attempt to protect them from deer browsing. The forest is a rich array of very familiar tree species including ash, hazel, hornbeam, oak, Norway spruce, silver fir and sycamore. A total of 30 trees were sampled from both populations, which has resulted in 175 trees being planted in the Yew Conservation Hedge.

PORTUGAL

Natural forests of yew are relatively common in the Iberian Peninsula, especially in northern parts of Spain; however, in Portugal they are extremely scarce. Here they only survive in Serra do Gerês in the north-east corner of the country and in Serra da Estrela in central Portugal. Of these two locations it is the latter that was chosen for the Yew Conservation Hedge, due to it being the most threatened. Dr Alexandre Silva, from the Serra da Estrela Interpretation Centre, advised on the location and the status of the yew population.

At a height of 1,993 metres, the Serra da Estrela is Portugal's highest mountain range, although it does not have a distinctive summit, but rather the highest point is a plateau that is accessible by a good road. All that remain are 40–50 mature trees and, although protected within the Serra da Estrela Natural Park of over 100,000 hectares, ironically this is still Portugal's most fire-prone mountain. For example, in 2005 a fire destroyed almost 80 per cent of the yew population. The remaining old-growth trees are highly fragmented; the largest group is a copse of four or five trees. What is of great concern is the lack of regeneration throughout the entire population, and without some sort of conservation intervention measures the yew could be lost altogether.

It was only possible to find six trees from which to collect seed, and this has resulted in 39 trees being planted in the Hedge. Crucially, recent in-country conservation measures are now being taken through the LIFE *Taxus* initiative. This is funded by Natura 2000, a European ecological conservation network, and the LIFE Programme of the European Union, which aims to restore native yew forests of the Mediterranean including those in Serra da Estrela. To date 15,000 trees have been planted, of which 40 per cent are yew trees which originate as seed collected from local populations. The project is also urgently addressing fire control by reducing the combustible load of the vegetation on the mountain.

RUSSIA

The Western Caucasus has some of the largest populations of
European yew, with very extensive stands in Sochi National Park
in south-western Caucasus, which forms part of the Western
Caucasus World Heritage Site. Covering an area of 190,000
hectares, the Park is located on the southern slopes of the main
Caucasian Ridge, which stretches along the Black Sea, from the
River Psou in the south-east to the Shepsi River near to Tuapse in
the north-west.

In September 2011 Richard Brown travelled to the town of Sochi
where he met up with Dr Boris Tuniyev, the Deputy Director of
the Federal State Institution Sochi National Park. Dr Tuniyev, a
passionate herpetologist, had gained a good knowledge of the forests
in the Park when searching for reptiles, especially for his beloved
snakes. His speciality is in shield-headed viper snakes, a new species
of which has been named in his honour. The area in and around
Sochi was very busy with new infrastructure being put in place ready
for the Winter Olympics Games, which were due to start in five
months' time – it was a relief to get into some wonderful old-growth
forests, set against some stunning limestone mountains.

Together, the two yew stands of Sochi and Khosta yew-box grove
encompass an area of almost 500 hectares. These stands are
thought to have remained relatively unchanged for the past
30 million years and contain massive trees, some reaching heights
of up to 30 metres. These forests have been closely monitored
since 1936; regeneration is generally good, but this tends to be in
lighter areas away from the canopy of the trees. The trees, which
often occur in small groups or as scattered individuals, favour the
valley bottoms close to watercourses where there is more humidity.
The associated vegetation varied from location to location, but
hornbeam and beech were especially frequent. The yew-box grove

is a well-known location for yews, but due to the box tree moth there has been a steep decline in the box forests of the Caucasus – it was all too clear to see the loss of box here in these forests. The healthy yew forests yielded an excellent crop of fruiting trees, which are now represented in the Yew Conservation Hedge by 28 individuals.

SWEDEN

The distribution of yew in Sweden is restricted to coastal forested areas in the southern part of the country where the oceanic influence yields relatively high rainfall and milder winters. One may think of yew as being resistant to low winter temperatures, and while this is broadly true, the lack of naturally occurring yews in the far north of Sweden (and Norway) suggests that there are limitations to its cold tolerance. Certainly, yew cannot match that of other native conifers such as Norway spruce and Scots pine, which can occur in the subarctic forests of Scandinavia.

There were many options when it came to choosing which Swedish yew population to collect seed from for the Yew Conservation Hedge. In the end, preference was given to a small forest on the well-known limestone island of Öland. This long, narrow strip of land in the Baltic Sea lies off the south-east coast of mainland Sweden and is the country's second-largest island. Yew is restricted to the island's northernmost point in the 5,800-hectare Böda Ecopark. This is a wilderness of barren sand dunes, pine forests and meadowlands, and within it is a further protected area called Idegransreservatet, which is an isolated forest of yew trees. The island is one of Sweden's most popular holiday resorts; therefore, the trees need all the protection they can be given.

The yew trees, which can be as much as eight metres tall, are within a coniferous forest dominated by mature Norway spruce and Scots pine, and where, on the margins of the forest, yew becomes more dominant as an understory tree. Here many trees have branches down to the ground where they have become layered and thrown up new shoots, and as a result these areas have become impenetrable. Tom Christian collected seed in 2009 from ten trees, and noted that in a period of just three years there has been a noticeable deterioration in the health of the forest. The cause of this is mainly due to invasive non-native species such as Western red cedar from North America casting heavy shade, which is preventing regeneration. To exacerbate the problem further, seed production is noticeably very low.

Ironically, because the area is designated as a nature reserve, the Swedish authorities encourage a non-intervention management policy. All nature reserves need to be managed and in this case the removal of non-native species to allow sufficient light is essential for the future survival of the yew forest. The good news is that the Yew Conservation Hedge is acting as a haven for 63 trees from this forest.

UKRAINE

In Ukraine the distribution of yew is limited to the Carpathian and Crimean Mountains. In the former it shares a greater distribution with its neighbouring countries of Poland, Romania and Slovakia, and it is here where the largest Ukrainian population in the Kniazhdvir Nature Reserve occurs with about 22,000 individuals. However, the collections for the Yew Conservation Hedge were made from the southern Crimea where over 3,000 trees are known from four main populations. Richard Brown travelled to Crimea in September 2011 where he was joined by Dr Vladimir Isikov from the Nikita Botanic Garden near Yalta. While visiting,

Richard's appetite for visiting the yew trees in their native habitat was whetted by seeing a 100-year-old yew tree growing in the Botanic Garden.

Seed was collected from several locations including Chatyr Dag Mountain, where there are groves of yew trees on the eastern side of the lower plateau. The most spectacular location visited was the Grand Canyon, which is often referred to as one of the wonders of the Crimean Peninsula. The three-kilometre-long canyon has a depth of 320 metres, but incredibly the width at the bottom is only two to three metres in places. Snaking its way through the canyon are the crystal-clear waters of the River Auzun-Uzen – in places water erosion has formed cauldrons and gullies that look more like porcelain sinks. The river has helped to create a very humid environment, perfect to sustain the yew trees growing above on steep slopes where they cling to the gorge sides, composed of peculiarly coloured limestone rock. The yews, some of which are eight metres tall, occur as scattered individuals or in small groups growing with oak and beech. The seed collections have resulted in 65 trees being planted in the Yew Conservation Hedge.